Give Them
an Argument

Logic for the Left

Give Them
an Argument

Logic for the Left

Ben Burgis

Winchester, UK
Washington, USA

JOHN HUNT PUBLISHING

First published by Zero Books, 2019
Zero Books is an imprint of John Hunt Publishing Ltd., No. 3 East St., Alresford,
Hampshire SO24 9EE, UK
office@jhpbooks.com
www.johnhuntpublishing.com
www.zero-books.net

For distributor details and how to order please visit the 'Ordering' section on our website.

ISBN: 978 1 78904 210 8
978 1 78904 211 5 (ebook)
Library of Congress Control Number: 2018964433

A CIP catalogue record for this book is available from the British Library.

Design: Stuart Davies

UK: Printed and bound by CPI Group (UK) Ltd, Croydon, CR0 4YY
US: Printed and bound by Thomson-Shore, 7300 West Joy Road, Dexter, MI 48130

We operate a distinctive and ethical publishing philosophy in
all areas of our business, from our global network of authors to
production and worldwide distribution.

To my beautiful wife Jennifer—among her many virtues, she's
the best logic instructor I know

I. The Milkman Fallacy and the Governor's Fallacy: Why Logic and Leftism Don't Always Seem to Mix

At the end of the spring semester, I went to a Philosophy Department party at Rutgers. A graduate student told me that she'd been assigned to teach a class called "Logic, Reasoning, and Persuasion" in the fall. She expressed amazement and confusion about the fact that it was "below" Rutgers' introductory symbolic logic class. What, she asked, could be below that? What did one even cover in such a class? Having taught LRP before, I said it was basically what other universities call a "Critical Reasoning" class. Whether it was because she was a little drunk or because the course is called something else in her native Canada, she still seemed to be drawing a blank. I suggested "fallacies," and this graduate student—a *Jacobin*-reading leftist who I agree with about most subjects—looked at me like I'd just suggested that she kill her cat. "God no," she said. "That's how people learn to become *annoying* libertarian *boys*."

Two years earlier, at a party for protestors and Bernie Sanders delegates at the Democratic National Convention hosted by the Philadelphia branch of the Democratic Socialists of America, I briefly met Will Menaker, Felix Biederman and Matt Christman. They told me I should check out their podcast. One of them gave me a business card. Within a few months, it became so popular that the hosts didn't have to do anything else for a living. In the summer of 2016, though, I had to check that business card to remember the name of the podcast—Chapo Trap House.

I gave it a listen. It traffics in exactly the kind of obnoxiously guy-ish humor the Canadian grad student would presumably dislike. I see why, but I have enough of a soft spot for that kind of thing that I get excited when a new Bill Burr or Doug Stanhope album comes out. I found the way they combined that sensibility with an aggressive and often insightful critique of centrist media figures and right-wing blowhards refreshing. I listened to the most recent episode and then I went back and listened from the beginning.

On Episode One, after some opening mockery of the earnest liberalism of Citizen Radio, the hosts kicked things off with "introductions." Each of them included a swipe or two at the assorted clowns and reactionaries they'd tangled with on Twitter.

Will: "To tell you a little about myself, I love coffee, dogs, big time movie guy, and I'm really into neo-feudalism and amateur phrenology—blood, soil, and tradition."

Felix: "Faves are pejorative, lists are to keep track of my favorites, retweets are not an endorsement, and my son is dead."

Matt: "I'm sort of the Midwest correspondent to talk to the rootless cosmopolitan New Yorkers on the team. The only thing I love more than a hot sizzling plate of bacon is proving people wrong by their own..."

Later, producer Brendan James came on board and the podcast started sounding smooth and professional. The guys produced this first episode by recording a Google Hangout session, and things were spotty at best. Matt's voice had cut out. It didn't matter. Even then, the joke was familiar enough that Will could pick it up where Matt had left off. "Their own logic? Have we lost Matt?"

After some dead air and heavy breathing, Matt came back. Pretty soon, everyone was riffing on the same theme, merrily naming imaginary logical fallacies.

Felix: "If you are employing the Milkman Fallacy, the Governor's Fallacy, any of them, we will not hesitate to call you on it."

Will: "There's nothing I like better than reducing simpletons and libtards to a quivering pile of their own urine and soiled garments when I just *slay* them with logic."

Mockery of people who talk a lot about logic has been a

staple of the show ever since. When, like their non-socialist predecessors at *The Daily Show* and *The Colbert Report*, the Chapo crew inevitably got around to putting out a book based on the show, it was subtitled *A Manifesto Against Logic, Facts, and Reason*.

To lay my biases on the table, I'm someone who talks a lot about logic. I'm a philosophy professor. My doctoral dissertation was about logical paradoxes, also the subject of my book *Logic Without Gaps or Gluts*. I've taught both symbolic logic and the dreaded "fallacy" class on many occasions and I think that (when they're done right) such courses serve a useful purpose.

Logic is the study of the ways in which the premises of arguments can support their conclusions—or, in the case of arguments that commit fallacies, the ways in which they can subtly fail to support those conclusions. To *prove someone wrong by their own logic* is to show that the assumptions they make in one context logically entail conclusions that they would reject in another. The fancy Latin name for an argument of this form is **Reductio Ad Absurdum**. If we see the process of logical argumentation as a collective search for truth rather than an attempt to reduce opponents to quivering piles of urine and soiled garments, an apparently successful **Reductio** argument against your position is only the beginning of the discussion. One possibility is to confront the (sometimes humbling) possibility that you were wrong, go back to the drawing board, and try again. This isn't the same as accepting that your opponent is right about everything. If you hold two positions that can't both be true, that means you're wrong about *something*. There's still an open question about which part you got wrong. And an apparently successful **Reductio** argument doesn't necessarily show that you got anything wrong at all. It could be that, when you dig a little deeper into the issue, you can show that your positions aren't really inconsistent at all. Showing this involves carefully explaining why two assumptions that seem similar are really different.

Not only can this process of disambiguation and clarification be a useful intellectual exercise that can help you better understand your own views, it can help you do a better job of communicating and explaining them to others. *That's* surely something that socialists need to do. Now that the authoritarian "socialism" of the Soviet bloc has receded into the historical rearview mirror, the prospects for the real thing have started to look more promising than they have for a long time. Even so, we face a steep uphill battle. More than a few Bernie Sanders voters harbored doubts about some of his more ambitious policy proposals. Once we get beyond those social democratic basics and start to consider an actual break from capitalism, the numbers get grim. Within our self-selected social media friends lists, we can agree with each other to our hearts' content about everything from prison abolition to Fully Automated Luxury Communism, but the fact remains that only a small percentage of the workers of the world are on board. One would think that the left would love anything that helped us present our ideas in a clearer and more plausible way. As two nineteenth century German philosophy majors wrote at the end of their Manifesto, we have a world to win!

So, how did so many leftists become so manifestly hostile to the very mention of logic? The phenomenon can't be reduced to one cause. One relatively esoteric part of the answer is the confusion about "dialectical logic" and its relationship to the kind of logic I'm talking about in this book that was introduced to the American socialist movement by Leon Trotsky in the 1930s. We'll get to that later in the book. Some bigger and more obvious pieces of the puzzle have to do with the toxic culture of social media, the ways in which logic is often taught at the introductory level, and the rhetorical posture of the right.

Realistically, anyone who non-ironically brags about having *proven someone wrong* by his or her *own logic* isn't likely to see argumentation as any sort of disinterested rational enterprise.

He or she—let's be honest, *he*—is far more likely to talk about logic as a sort of mental weapon he can use to defeat and humiliate "libtards." Even the words "logic" and "argument" are wielded almost like magical talismans with mysterious powers to reduce opponents to quivering piles of urine and soiled garments. Post a video critical of the alt-right in certain online spaces and you'll be greeted by a hundred comments smarmily or angrily claiming that the video is "not an argument." One of the more bizarre creations of Trump-loving editorial cartoonist Ben Garrison was a cartoon depicting Trump-loving podcaster Stefan Molyneux using needles labeled "logic," "reason," and "evidence" to puncture balloons as an oddly thin and muscular version of Donald Trump watches approvingly. Each balloon contains a screaming face. An angry black man who might be meant to represent Barack Obama says, "Trump is Hitler!" An angry elephant says, "Never Trump!" An angry Megan Kelly says, "Trump is a misogynist!" Other, less recognizable figures yell, "Trump is a racist!", "Trump went bankrupt!", and "My feelings!" As a smiling Molyneux punctures them all, he proclaims, "Not an argument!"

While it's certainly true that a three or four word summary of an assertion like "Trump is a misogynist" is not in itself an *argument* either *for* that claim or *from* it to some other conclusion, it's somewhat mysterious why Garrison takes this to be a damning criticism. (I imagine him walking around his house late at night, angrily accusing his lamp and his toaster and his household pets of not being arguments.) Pointing out that something is "not an argument" is itself not an argument. It could perhaps be *part* of an implied argument, but no serious attempt to reconstruct what that looks like would make it look like a *good* argument. If the first premise is that most assertions of Trump's misogyny aren't backed up by explicit arguments and the implied conclusion is that the people doing the asserting are irrational, what does Premise Two look like? It seems like it would have to be something like this:

Premise Two: It's irrational to ever assert anything about anything without immediately laying out your reasons for holding that position in the form an explicit argument.

Taken seriously, this gives rise to an infinite regress problem. If you want to assert Premise Two, you'd better back *that* up with an explicit argument, and back up each of the premises you use in *that* argument with an explicit argument, *and...and...* Good luck with that.

Of course, the "not an argument" brigades don't seriously advocate this standard. Labeling everything under the sun as *NOT AN ARGUMENT* is their way of signaling that they're superior to the irrational left-wing scum.

In this environment, it almost goes without saying that claims of inconsistency aren't being used to push people to think more deeply about their apparently conflicting positions. When Ben Shapiro insinuates on Twitter that anyone who supports anti-discrimination ordinances that prevent fundamentalist bakers from refusing to make gay wedding cakes and also approves of restaurants refusing service to Trump Administration officials is being inconsistent and instructs us to "pick one," he isn't inviting thoughtful responses. He doesn't want his Twitter followers to reflect on the reasons why some categories but not others form the basis of "protected classes" for the purposes of anti-discrimination laws and whether those considerations could reasonably be applied to the "class" of government officials with unpopular policies. He just wants the liberals and leftists hate-reading his Twitter feed to feel momentarily confused and defensive and unsure of themselves before he moves on to his next point. The best outcome for him would be for someone to call him a homophobe, so he can respond with his catchphrase, "Facts don't care about your feelings."

Star Trek having given generations of American television viewers the very mistaken idea that "logic" has something to do with being "unemotional" — more on that in Chapter II — both free market libertarians and creepy online ethnonationalists delight in contrasting their investment in "facts" and "logic" with the left's alleged obsession with "emotions." Many leftists quite correctly sense that the point of this rhetorical strategy is to turn a disturbing lack of empathy with the victims of right-wing policies into a virtue. Once you've been told enough times that you wouldn't object to human rights violations in Palestine or on America's southern border if you were less "emotional" and hence more "logical," it's only natural to start to wonder whether there's something very wrong with anyone who makes a big deal of valorizing logic.

I'm genuinely excited about the renewed socialist left that's coalesced around organizations like the Democratic Socialists of America, magazines like *Jacobin* and *Current Affairs*, and podcasts like Chapo Trap House and The Michael Brooks Show. I wouldn't claim, though, that it currently adds up to a mass movement of the most exploited portions of the American working class. At the moment, it's disproportionately composed of a quasi-privileged stratum of college-educated urbanites. (*Quasi*-privileged because such an education has ceased to be a guarantee of much of anything about someone's economic future other than that it will include decades of paying down student loan debt. I don't think I'm breaking any new ground when I suggest that this situation played a non-trivial role in the revival of the left.) Enough universities require some sort of introductory Logic or Critical Reasoning class that many *Jacobin* readers and Chapo listeners who chuckle along with the swipes at logicbros have had the experience of learning to distinguish valid and invalid argument forms and identify short passages as examples of **Ad Hominem**, **Begging the Question**, and other fallacies.

As is true for everything from Algebra to English Literature, these classes can be taught well or badly. Examinations of valid and invalid forms often focus on stock examples that bear little resemblance to the complexities of interesting real world debates. One of the first argument forms covered in any introductory logic class is **Modus Ponens**:

> Premise One: If P, then Q.
> Premise Two: P.
> Conclusion: Q.

The next is likely to be **Modus Tollens**:

> Premise One: If P, then Q.
> Premise Two: Not-Q.
> Conclusion: Not-P.

The particular Ps and Qs used to illustrate these argument forms often have a strange and slightly artificial feel. One might illustrate **Modus Ponens**, for example, with an example drawn from current affairs.

Premise One: If Donald Trump won the election, then a Republican won the election.

Premise Two: Donald Trump won the election.

Conclusion: A Republican won the election.

A slight variation of the example might be tweaked to illustrate an invalid argument form, like **Asserting the Consequent**.

Premise One: If P, then Q.

Premise Two: Q.

Conclusion: P.

For example:

Premise One: If Ted Cruz won the election, then a Republican

won the election.
Premise Two: A Republican won the election.
Conclusion: Ted Cruz won the election.

Modus Ponens and **Modus Tollens** are valid argument forms, meaning that it's logically impossible to construct an argument with one of those forms in which the premises are all true and the conclusion is false. Such an argument can never take you from truth to falsity. That doesn't necessarily mean that if confronted with an argument with a valid form, you should roll over and accept the conclusion. After all, one of the premises might be false! It does, however, tell you that if you accept all the premises and reject the conclusion, you have an inconsistent set of beliefs. As with our discussion of **Reductio Ad Absurdum** above, that shows that you must have gone wrong *somewhere*. If you want to arrive at the truth, this is useful information to have. It's also useful to know that **Asserting the Consequent**, though it might *look* like a valid argument, can be used to take you from true premises to false conclusions.

The problem, the reason all of this feels so artificial, is that no one in real life would feel the need to *argue* for a conclusion that everyone knew was true (like "A Republican is President") or that everyone knew was false (like "Ted Cruz is President"). Even if they did, they certainly wouldn't bother to spell out the if-then premise.

None of this necessarily adds up to a critique of this way of introducing the material. The idea is to set up the far more formally complicated material the class will be grappling with for the rest of the semester by quickly communicating a complex set of ideas about truth, validity, reasoning, and the relationship between the three concepts. In this context, simplistic stock examples have their place. Even so, some students might be left with the understandable impression that logic is a sort of formal game that can only be played with silly and simplistic examples divorced from real reasoning.

This problem gets even more pronounced when it comes to informal fallacies like **Appeal to Authority** and **Ad Hominem**. Many textbooks present the subject in a very superficial way, and even many otherwise good professors test students on it in a way that compounds the problem. The **Appeal to Authority** fallacy is committed when "Impressive Person P endorses Conclusion C" is treated as a reason to believe C despite the fact that P's impressiveness gives P no special expertise on anything relevant to C. Albert Einstein was a leftist. He even wrote an article called "Why Socialism?" that appeared in the May 1949 issue of *Monthly Review*. That's an interesting historical tidbit. As a socialist, I enjoy knowing that Comrade Albert was on the right side of history. "Einstein was a socialist" would, however, be a very bad *reason* to support socialism. Werner Heisenberg was both a great physicist and enough of a blindly loyal German patriot that he doesn't seem to have had any moral qualms about trying to build an atomic bomb for Hitler.

Ad Hominem is the other side of the same coin—the mistake in reasoning we make when we take "Vile Person P believes Conclusion C" as a reason to reject C. Richard Spencer supports universal healthcare and opposes U.S. airstrikes in Syria. I wouldn't invite him to speak at an anti-war rally or a Medicare for All panel, but any "woke" neoliberal centrist who took Spencer's positions to somehow bolster the case for Obamacare or liberal interventionism *should* be called on their use of fallacious reasoning.

The problem is that learning the definitions of these fallacies is far easier than exercising judgment about when they've been committed. When I've taught informal logic classes (like Critical Reasoning or the aforementioned "LRP" class at Rutgers), I've seen that a little logic can be a dangerous thing. If you test students on their ability to match up short passages in which some fallacy is definitely committed with a list of names of fallacies, many will do quite well. If you ask the same students to go out and find examples of fallacies being committed "in the wild" in opinion pieces and blog posts, many of the same students will turn up false positives. Any citation of expert opinion will be classified as Appeal to Authority. Any example of *saying something mean* will be classified as **Ad Hominem**. Even though a "fallacy" is by definition a way that an *argument* goes wrong so that the premises don't really support the conclusion, fallacy-happy students can somehow find "fallacies" even in passages in which no arguments are made.

I've come to believe that the best way to teach this material is to spend a small portion of the unit on teaching students the definitions of a handful of fallacies and the rest of it having them practice identifying them "in the wild" so the false positives can be corrected again and again. Otherwise, me and my fellow logic instructors are complicit in the creation of monsters—the legion of basement dwelling libertarians, neo-reactionaries, and even stranger beasts who've learned to respond to all objections to their views by rattling off accusation after accusation that their opponents have committed this or that fallacy. When a relatively normal person tangles with such a creature in online spaces, they're not likely to devote the time and energy that would be required to carefully and thoroughly address these accusations one at a time. Instead, they might respond with a bit of snark or by simply cutting their losses and ending the conversation. This is, of course, what the right-wing logicbro wants. It allows him to do a victory lap, relishing in the way his "butthurt" opponent has been demolished by the power of his logical skills.

Contrapoints, a left-wing transwoman (and philosophy grad school dropout) who often tangles with the alt-right on her YouTube channel, has a particularly funny video called "Everyone's a Little Bit Racist Sometimes (A Response to ArmouredSkeptic)." ArmouredSkeptic is exactly what he sounds like—someone who (a) takes his atheism to make him an exemplar of rationality and (b) is pretty sure that racism is not a problem. After the previous interaction between Contra and Armoured, one of Armoured's fans on Twitter exulted about how Armoured had "annihilated" Contra. "He went in on you like there was no tomorrow, as if we were on the brink of extinction... Raw, unannounced, no lube, just ripped your faggoty as[s] panties apart and came all over you." In the "A Little Bit Racist" video, Contra reads off the tweet and asks, "Is tearing your opponent's butthole to shreds really the aim of rationality? I always thought the purpose of rational argument was communication, or even, y'know, reaching some kind of mutual understanding, not just annihilating a human being. Socrates wasn't arguing with the citizens of Athens because he wanted to blast their buttholes... ok, actually, he did want to do that...but wasn't there also a thing about, like, truth...?"

That love of logic doesn't always thrive in this environment is not shocking. Even Contra's critique, though, points to a final reason why some on the left have learned to distrust the people who are most interested in talking about arguments. The idea that we should be aiming at "reaching a mutual understanding" with our political opponents can smack of the "anti-ideological" sermons frequently preached by neoliberal centrists. Certain writers at *The Atlantic* and *The New York Times* love to accuse any leftist intemperate and uncivil enough to use the word "oppression" of wanting to defeat their enemies instead of reasoning with them to find mutually agreeable "solutions" to society's problems. Any number of vapid David Brooks columns and Jonathan Chait essays have been based on this premise. More insidiously, so was Barack Obama's futile first term search for a "Grand Bargain" with Congressional Republicans to balance the budget and "save" entitlements by slashing them.

Leftists are absolutely right to reject this centrist vision. It is dangerously naïve to believe that political disagreements always or even usually boil down to people with the same goals talking past each other or failing to be calm and civil enough to reason together about how to get there. We have different goals because we have different values and, at the base of political conflict, different *interests*. At the end of the day, I'm a Marxist. I don't think there's some moral argument that will persuade the people who own and control the means of production to turn them over to the working class without a fight. Nor do I believe that all members of the working class can be persuaded. Don't waste too many hours arguing with the guy at your workplace who rants about how the Border Patrol should just be allowed to kill "wetbacks." If your union is preparing to vote on a resolution condemning Trump's immigration policies, that guy needs to be isolated and defeated. Don't mistake the book you're holding for a plea for civility. Incivility in itself doesn't bother me—I think Chapo is hilarious—and I'm under no illusion that even basic concessions like healthcare and a living wage can be wrung out of the ruling class without a lot of entirely uncivil political struggle. I don't even disagree that, when they're used in a wise and targeted manner, social shaming tactics have their place.

That said, a left that *only* knows how to shame, call out, privilege-check, and diagnose the allegedly unsavory motivations of people who disagree with us will lose a lot of persuadable people whose material interests should put them on our side. What's more, left-wing people who really do share all the same long-term goals often find themselves disagreeing about strategy and tactics. Should we advocate a Universal Jobs Guarantee (UJG) or Universal Basic Income (UBI)? Or are all demands for radical reforms within the current system counterproductive distractions from the fight against capitalism itself? Should social democrats and socialists try to form a labor party? Can we take over the Democratic Party? Should we just focus on non-electoral activism? These are complicated questions. If we're out of practice using the kind of reasoning skills enhanced and sharpened by the study of logic, if we find that we're just *better* at privilege-checking and snark and diagnosing people's motivations than we are at making compelling arguments for our positions, the inevitable consequence is that when we argue with each other about these points of intra-left disagreement, all of those weapons are turned inward. That kind of thing makes the left about as appealing to potential converts as an endless Twitter war about race science with toxic right-wing logicbros. We can do better.

II. Facts Don't Care About Your Feelings: Ben Shapiro vs. David Hume

In a famous passage at the end of Section I, Part I of his 1738 *Treatise of Human Nature,* David Hume complains about reading books where "the author proceeds for some time in the ordinary way of reasoning and establishes the being of a God, or makes observations concerning human affairs; when of a sudden I am supriz'd to find" that the author has switched from speaking of "is and is not" to speaking of "ought and ought not" even though it seems "altogether impossible" that claims about what ought to be can be "a deduction from" claims about what is, "which are of an entirely different kind."

Evaluative conclusions (i.e. conclusions about what *should* happen, or about what's good or bad, right or wrong, admirable or detestable) can't be derived from purely factual premises. This principle is sometimes called **Hume's Law**. Let's put a pin in that while we talk about Ben Shapiro.

In an oddly gushing profile in the liberal *New York Times*, Sabrina Tavernise calls Shapiro the "destroyer of weak arguments." Tavernise emphasizes the overwhelming maleness of Shapiro's audience, and pushes back—albeit under the cover of "critics say"—against his characterization of "straight white males" as victims of "the left." Nowhere, however, does she so much as hint that anyone anywhere doubts that Shapiro is a formidable logical "gladiator."

Certainly, this is how he likes to present himself. His bestselling 2014 booklet on argumentation is entitled, "How to Debate Leftists and Destroy Them: 11 Rules for Winning the Argument." One imagines a hapless Noam Chomsky having to be carried out of a college auditorium on a stretcher after being *destroyed* in a debate with Ben Shapiro.

In the *New York Times* profile, David French assures us that

Shapiro doesn't just indiscriminately destroy everything in sight.

> Mr. French calls Mr. Shapiro a "principled gladiator." His aggressive tone draws in audiences, he said, but he does not attack unfairly, stoke anger for the sake of it, or mischaracterize his opponents' positions.

Even though Tavernise's profile emphasizes Shapiro's prowess as a debater, she only gives us one instance of Shapiro in action as the Destroyer of Weak Arguments.

> People often discover Mr. Shapiro by seeing a video clip of him arguing with somebody. Some have been watched millions of times, like one from a college in Michigan in February. After a back and forth with a young woman in the audience about transgenderism, Mr. Shapiro asked her how old she was. She said 22.
>
> "Why aren't you 60?" he asked. "What is the problem with you identifying as 60?"
>
> The young woman looked at him and hesitated, lowering the microphone slightly.
>
> "It's not the same as gender," she said. "You can't just ..."
>
> Mr. Shapiro looked at her, his face impassive: "You're right," he said. "You can't magically change your gender. You can't magically change your sex. You can't magically change your age."
>
> [This is] vintage Shapiro. He takes apart arguments in ways that makes the conservative conclusion seem utterly logical, like putting a key in a locked door.

The first thing to notice about this exchange is that Shapiro is doing exactly what French says he never does. On Shapiro's account, trans people and their advocates think you can magically change your biological sex. Mischaracterizations of opponent's positions don't get much cruder than that. (As Nathan Robinson points out in his indispensable *Current Affairs* piece on Shapiro, "What people mean when they say that 'gender is a social construct' is not that 'chromosomes are a social construct' but that in practice, gender isn't reducible to chromosomes.") The second is that Shapiro's "utterly logical" destruction of his 22-year-old interlocutor consists of (a) Shapiro making an extremely dubious analogy, (b) the 22-year-old starting to say that these two things don't actually seem to her to be very similar, and (c) Shapiro cutting her off before she has a chance to explore any of the many relevant differences between the two cases.

Before thinking about how age and gender might be different, it's worth acknowledging that there are *some* similarities between those categories. There is an objective, non-socially constructed fact of the matter that the victim of Shapiro's "destruction" was 22 rather than 60. (To head off a possible confusion, the specific words and numbers we happen to use to describe ages are certainly culturally contingent, but the actual property of having existed for a certain amount of time has nothing to do with the particular system that some group of humans happen to use to *measure* time.) Similarly, trans rights advocates can and should concede that there are objective, non-socially-constructed facts about biological sex.

Granted, an extreme position exists according to which even sex is a social construct. It's true that some babies are born with chromosomal abnormalities or other conditions that result in unusual combinations of sexual characteristics (what's sometimes thought of as a third "intersex" category) but it doesn't follow from this fact that there isn't an objective biological distinction between the sexes. To see why, consider what logicians call the "Sorites Paradox." Take my bald-headed friend Dan Corrigan. Add a hair to his head. Is he still bald? Given the way we usually use the word "bald," he is. Add another hair. And another. And another and another and another until he looks like Fabio. At some point, Dan stopped being bald, but when? There will be plenty of cases that we aren't sure what to say about, but one of the lessons that most philosophers draw from the paradox is that we're making a mistake if we try to infer from the premises that ambiguous cases exist and it's hard to know where to draw the line to the conclusion that the distinction isn't real and there aren't unambiguous cases on both sides. The proper name for this mistake is the **Continuum Fallacy**.

As Robinson says, most trans rights activists *don't* make this mistake. To see why they don't need to argue in this way to make the case for dignity and equality, let's go back to Shapiro's analogy between age and gender. It's true that there are objective facts about age. It's true that there are objective facts about sex. But what about gender? One internally consistent way of using gendered language is to call any biologically male adult human a "man" and any biologically female adult human a "woman." This is not, however, the *only* internally consistent way to use these terms, or the way that's appropriate for every context.

Philosophy professor and trans activist Sophie Grace Chappell offers an analogy between transwomen (or transmen) and adoptive parents. As with "man" and "woman," there's an internally consistent way of using the words "parent," "mother," and "father" to only refer to a child's biological progenitors. There is, however, a social use of all of these terms that often coincides with the biological use but which comes apart from it in some cases. Someone who has the legal *role* of a father is a "father" in a well-understood sense even if he isn't a father in the sense at issue when a doctor says, "The tests came back and you're the father." Most people who are fathers in the first sense are also fathers in the second sense, but plenty of men are only one or the other. Most people who are "women" in the sense of identifying as women and presenting themselves to others as women are also biologically female human beings, but some people are only one or the other.

Of course, one's status as childless or a parent is in several respects unlike one's gender identity. (An adoptive parent, like a biological parent, is unlikely to have "seen themselves" as a parent back when they were arguing with their own parents about bedtime.) No analogy is perfect. If A is like B in *every* way, then A just *is* B and we're dealing not with an analogy but with an instance of the **Law of Identity**. (We'll explore that principle in Chapter IV.) However, Chappell's analogy is better than Shapiro's in at least two crucial ways. First, it's far from clear that there is more than one way of using phrases like "22 years old" and "60 years old" that's both internally consistent and maps onto any part of what are the ordinary meanings of these phrases. Second, Chappell's analogy at least hints at some of the ugly real world consequences of Shapiro's position. Any teacher who angrily refused to have parent-teacher conferences with adoptive parents on the grounds that they weren't "real" parents would be considered by decent people to be a strange and cruel bigot.

If Shapiro had any interest in reasoning about the nuances of these issues in a good-faith effort to discover the truth, he would have waited for the flustered 22-year-old to collect her thoughts so she could start articulating some of the disanalogies between gender and age. Rather transparently, though, that's not Shapiro's goal.

Here are the eleven rules from his booklet on arguing with leftists and *destroying them*:

#1: *Walk Toward the Fire*

"You have to take the punch, you have to brush it off. You have to be willing to take the punch."

#2: *Hit First*

"Don't take the punch first. Hit first. Hit hard. Hit where it counts…"

One plausible explanation of Shapiro's constant use of the punching metaphor is that he's a bad and lazy writer. Anyone who's ever read his political thriller *True Allegiance* (or even just listened to the extracts that Will Menaker has read aloud on Chapo Trap House) knows that, as a novelist, Shapiro makes Ayn Rand look like F. Scott Fitzgerald. Even so, it's worth thinking about what else might be going on here.

At the risk of being tediously pedantic, let's consider one or two possible disanalogies between a fistfight and a political debate. To start with, the purpose of a debate is, presumably, to convince someone somewhere of something. Otherwise, what's the point?

Of course, in a great many contexts your *opponent* won't change her mind. Even in the context of casual arguments among friends, it's rare for anyone to change his mind "in the room." It's very difficult in practice for most people to disentangle their egos from the positions they're defending *during* a conversation, even a relatively calm one. (As anyone who's ever been around philosophy professors and graduate students knows, even professional training in weighing the virtues of arguments doesn't do all that much to cut down on this problem. The best you can usually hope for there is a grudging, "That's an interesting point. I'll have to think about it.") It's easy to draw extreme conclusions from this observation. I've heard many people who clearly thought they were being insightful saying that no one *ever* changes their mind because of an argument. This view is as silly and psychologically shallow as the mistake you'd be making by expecting an opponent to change their mind in the room. People *do* change their minds all the time, and arguments can and do play a role in this process, sometimes because they gradually gnaw at the back of your mind and sometimes because after enough time has passed that your ego isn't bound up in some previously held position, you just realize to your own surprise that you now accept the contrary position for the very reasons that you dismissed when you first heard them.

Granted, even this is generally too much to hope for in less casual contexts. In 2017, Bhaskar Sunkara and Vivek Chibber from *Jacobin* debated Nick Gillespie and Katherine Mangu-Ward, editors of the libertarian magazine *Reason*. Presumably everyone involved went into the event not just knowing that none of their opponents would have a political epiphany on the stage, but that there was no realistic chance whatsoever that, for example, Gillespie might run into Sunkara a few months later and say, "You know, Bhaskar, I've had a chance to think it over and you're totally right about capitalism."

This isn't a knock on Nick Gillespie. A conversion in the other direction would be just as unlikely for all the same psychologically obvious reasons. When you're arguing with someone whose personal and professional worlds would be thrown into crisis if they came around to your point of view, or even just with your racist uncle who's deeply emotionally invested in what he's saying about immigration, convincing that person isn't going to be a realistic goal. If there's a worthwhile purpose to be served by engaging with them—and in the uncle case, there may not be—it's to convince persuadable observers.

One way of doing this, if the observers are gullible enough to fall for it, is to just rattle off superficially plausible-sounding points so quickly that no one has time to stop and think about them. If this is your strategy, then the analogy between a point made in a debate as a punch thrown in a fistfight makes perfect sense. If an opponent has their guard down, like the 22-year-old momentarily flustered by Shapiro's specious comparison of gender identity to age, you should keep hitting them. Otherwise, they might recover their equilibrium and hit you back! Again, and at the risk of beating to death a point that's already been made, this is the opposite of how you should act if you actually want to make sure that your argument is a good one and your conclusion is true. If you want *that*, you need to slow the hell down and think through possible objections.

#3: *Frame Your Opponent*

Leftists, Shapiro says, always characterize conservatives as being horrible bigots. You, conservative reader, should get out ahead of this by preemptively characterizing your opponent as untrustworthy! "There is no way to convince someone that you don't hate him or her. You *can* convince them, however, that the opposition is a liar and a hater."

He goes on to make the amazing claim that the reason the GOP consistently loses the black and Hispanic vote is "not because the right's policies are so abhorrent to blacks and Hispanics, but because blacks and Hispanics have been told for generations that conservatives hate them." (There's a reason he cites no polling data to back up this assertion. At least on economic issues, all the actual data shows that these populations are well to the left of the *Democratic* Party, never mind the Republicans.)

Shapiro assures us that this "I'm not a racist, you're a liar" move has a high-minded purpose. "[T]he only way to get beyond character arguments is to frame your opponent – make it toxic for your opponent to slur you. Then, hopefully, you can move the debate to more substantive territory."

Maybe. On the other hand, even a casual perusal of Shapiro's body of work strongly suggests an alternative explanation. *True Allegiance* includes scenes where radical black agitators speaking a strange and hopelessly dated "jive talk" conspire to lure an innocent policeman into killing an unarmed black teen as a kind of false flag operation to make the police look racist. In his non-fiction work, he routinely mocks the idea that racial injustice has anything to do with the massive wealth gap between white and black Americans. And when it comes to the group he gets most worked up about—"Arabs" in general and Palestinians in particular—his feelings are a lot less subtle than that.

In an article entitled, "The Radical Evil of the Palestinian Arab Population," Shapiro writes that, "The problem runs deeper than a few figureheads. The Palestinian Arab population is rotten to the core." This is, he says, "the most evil population on the planet." In the past, he's suggested that *all* of these people—not just the three million Palestinian adults and children living in the West Bank and the two million in Gaza but the 1.6 million ethnically Palestinian citizens of "Israel proper"—be forcibly removed from their homes. To be fair, he's backtracked about that part—a bit. He now refers to his former advocacy of outright ethnic cleansing as an "error," averring that such a mass transfer would be "inhumane and impractical."

Inference to the Best Explanation (IBE) is a method of reasoning that involves comparing different theories that are all technically consistent with the data to see which one is the simplest, most explanatory, least *ad hoc*, and so on. Let's see if we can apply that here. It's possible that Shapiro's backtracking about ethnic cleansing only *sounds* so half-hearted—"inhumane and impractical"—because he's experimenting with expressing himself in a far more understated way than he ever has in any of his previous writing. It's also possible that his concern for taking the issue of racism off the table comes from a high-minded desire to move discussions "to more substantive territory." In both cases, though, these may not be the most convincing explanations.

#4: *Frame the Argument*

The left always "frames the debate" with "buzzwords" like "tolerance" and "social justice." Shapiro advises his readers not to fall for it. Instead of arguing about whether it is "unjust" or "intolerant" to deny legal recognition to same-sex marriages, for example, he recommends making leftists debate "why marriage should be redefined, and how this will strengthen the institution."

A useful exercise for anyone actually curious about how to answer *those* questions would be to ask the same questions about the Supreme Court's 1967 *Loving v. Virginia* ruling banning southern states from defining marriage as a union of one man and one woman of the same race. (Does moving to a definition loose enough to allow for interracial marriage "strengthen the institution?" What exactly does that mean? If extending marriage rights to mixed race couples *didn't* strengthen marriage, should the state of Virginia have been allowed to carry on refusing recognition to such unions?) More importantly for our purposes, though, notice that Shapiro—the NYT-anointed Destroyer of Weak Arguments—isn't talking about how to refute justice-based arguments for marriage equality by identifying dubious premises or by showing some flaw in the reasoning typically used to get from those premises to the conclusion that legal marriage should be available to same sex-couples. He's advising conservatives to change the subject.

Similarly, neither *walk toward the fire* nor *hit first* has anything to do with arguments per se. Neither does *frame your opponent*. Skipping #5 for a moment, neither does…

#6: *Force Leftists to Answer Questions*

…or:

#7: *Do Not Get Distracted*

…or:

#8: *You Do Not Have to Defend People on Your Side*

…or:

#9: *If You Don't Know Something, Admit It*

…or:

#10: *Let the Other Side Have Meaningless Victories*

…or:

#11: *Body Language Matters*

To be clear, there's nothing wrong with paying careful attention to the rhetorical half of presenting arguments. I often wish that my fellow leftists cared more about getting that part right. It is striking, though, that Ben Shapiro, allegedly a "logic machine," only devotes one of his eleven rules to the actual evaluation of arguments.

#5: *Spot Inconsistencies in the Left's Arguments*

He gives two examples—although, as we'll see, he does

gesture in the general direction of a couple others. First, leftists "say they want to ban assault weapons to stop gun murders. But that argument is silly, because handguns are used to kill far more people than so-called assault weapons" and "the left" doesn't support an outright handgun ban.

Secondly, leftists advocate a "right" to healthcare, but don't advocate that the government require that "a certain percentage of the population go to medical school." He does strongly suggest that the left *really* wants to draft people into service as doctors — and ban handguns — but that it keeps this true agenda secret for fear of spooking the general public. The "inconsistency" claim is based on the policy preferences leftists *claim* to have, though, so in the interests of addressing that, we'll put the issue of a second, secret agenda to one side.

Start with gun control. If Shapiro ever talked to someone with politics to the left of Piers Morgan — and if he took a long enough break from screaming the names of logical fallacies in that person's face to actually listening to what they were saying — he might find out that the left is split on this issue. While it's true that even many socialists think that tightening up American gun laws to some approximation of what's already on the books in most first world countries would be a net positive, more than a few of their comrades worry that harsher gun laws would be disproportionately applied to poor black and brown offenders and that the objective effect of such laws would be to make America's mass incarceration epidemic even worse. At any rate, Shapiro's argument here seems to be directed not so much against the actual left as the sort of wishy-washy Clintonite liberals whose ideas about gun policy (like their ideas about most issues) are all about incremental tinkering around the edges of the problem.

Even against this target, Shapiro's objection falls flat. Hardly anyone claims that any particular gun control measure will eliminate all (or even most) gun violence. All they need to claim—and all they generally do claim—is that the proposal in question will reduce the *rate* of gun violence enough that, when weighed against any negative consequences that might come about as a result of the law, it's still a good idea. You could quite consistently believe, for example, that (a) the right to armed self-defense is important enough that it would be wrong to ban *all* guns, but (b) a narrow ban on the category of guns often dubbed "assault weapons" would save enough lives to be worth doing. Whether this is the *right* view is a complicated question that needs to be decided on the substantive merits of both claims, but Shapiro's critique is a textbook example of the **Nirvana Fallacy**—the logical leap from the premise that some plan of action won't *completely* solve the problem it's meant to address to the conclusion that there's no point in doing it. Murder and rape are regular occurrences in societies with laws against them, but it doesn't follow that there's no reason to keep those laws on the books. Nor is there anything inconsistent about saying that competing values should be weighed against each other. I think that the full range of recreational drugs should be legalized and regulated like alcohol, but I wouldn't accuse a conservative of "inconsistency" for supporting existing drug laws without advocating that the police be given the power to warrantlessly bust into private homes to drag away random citizens and force them to pee into cups.

The inconsistency claim about healthcare is even more obviously wrong. Earlier, we saw David French claim that Shapiro "does not attack unfairly...or mischaracterize his opponents' positions." Well, deliberate misunderstandings of opponents' positions don't get much more transparently silly than taking someone saying that every resident of the United States should have a legally guaranteed right to healthcare as saying that unwilling citizens should be pressed into service as doctors. The Supreme Court ruled in *Miranda v. Arizona* (1966) that criminal suspects have a right to legal representation. Is

Shapiro seriously confused about how this can be the law of the land if a certain percentage of the population isn't forced to go to law school? Shapiro himself presumably believes that we all have a right to police protection. Does that mean that he supports forcing some of his fellow citizens at gunpoint to attend their local police academies? If not, he has no excuse for pretending to misunderstand what leftists mean by "right" in this context.

I've seen people frame a variation of Shapiro's argument with thought experiments about small numbers of people stranded together on islands. If none of them are doctors and none have any interest in being doctors, what happened to the "right" to healthcare? Well, put four people on the island. Person 1 kills Person 2. Would Person 3 and Person 4—both close friends of Person 2—be justified in punishing Person 1 in some way for his crime? If so, what happened to the right not to be punished for one's crimes without a jury trial? The answer is that the right to a trial, like the right to healthcare, is inapplicable to this situation. What we mean when we say that people have rights of this kind is that, in a sufficiently developed society for it to be possible for the government to secure doctors or lawyers for everyone simply by footing the bill, failing to do so would be unjust.

Shapiro makes a final half-hearted attempt to gesture at a couple of other cases of left-wing inconsistency.

> Healthcare and gun control aren't the only examples. On same-sex marriage, the left claims that the state has no business regulating someone's private life...unless the left is simultaneously proclaiming that the state *must* sanction someone's private activity. On abortion, the left says it is for choice but ignores that the baby has no choice.

The first of these examples is almost impressively intellectually lazy. *Allowing* same-sex couples that want to enter into the legal institution of marriage to do so is hardly a violation of anyone's right to conduct their private lives as they see fit.

The abortion example is slightly better, but only very slightly. *If* everyone agreed that a fetus at the state of development when abortions generally take place was a full-fledged person with its own right to bodily autonomy, Shapiro's complaint would make at least some sense, but of course almost no one on the pro-choice side *does* grant that premise. Nor should they, considering that our best current evidence shows that the first flickering of electricity in the fetal brain doesn't happen until well into the second trimester. If a fetus is simply an insensate collection of cells that might one day *become* a person, there's nothing inconsistent about saying that people have moral rights that fetuses do not.

If you want to know how to defend a pro-choice conclusion even after accepting for the sake of argument that Shapiro's premise is true, read Judith Jarvis Thomson's classic article "A Defense of Abortion." Thomson is a careful and thoughtful writer. She makes rigorous arguments and then holds them up to the light to examine them for faults she may have missed. She's a joy to read.

The comparison to Shapiro doesn't need to be belabored. Suffice it to say that it's deeply unlikely that any left-wing reader of *How to Debate Leftists and Destroy Them* has ever felt particularly destroyed.

The real source of Shapiro's reputation as a Logical Superman of the Right probably has more to do with his observations about the relationship between "facts" and "feelings." Think back to the issue of Shapiro's insistence on referring to trans people by pronouns they reject, and Sophie Grace Chappell's analogy about trans people and adoptive parents. I said that someone who took a Shapiro-like stand toward adoptive parents, adamantly refusing to use words like "mother" and "father" in any but their biological senses, would be a "strange and cruel bigot."

A Shapiro fan might see grist in all of this for a Shapiroan lecture on facts and feelings. After all, Shapiro's stance is exclusively rooted in biological *facts* about sex. All this talk of "cruelty" smacks of *feelings*.

Shapiro's "facts don't care about your feelings" catchphrase has spread like wildfire among online conservatives. The faithful can buy "facts don't care about your feelings" t-shirts. They can drink their coffee in "facts don't care about your feelings" mugs. Anyone who wants to carry around all nine of Shapiro's books at once can transport them in a "facts don't care about your feelings" tote bag. The text of the slogan on the tote bag is accompanied by a white-on-black outline of a Kleenex box—for "liberal tears."

So…what exactly does Shapiro's catchphrase *mean*?

Facts presumably don't "care" about anything. They also don't reason with each other. They don't even correct people who misrepresent them. Human beings have to do that on their behalf. What's the point of saying that facts don't care about *feelings* in particular?

Uncharitably, we might conjecture that he just likes the sound of being pro-facts and anti-feelings and that that's about it. There does seem to be a bit more going on here, though—something that connects to his carefully cultivated reputation as the Destroyer of Weak Arguments.

Certainly, Shapiro's online fans are often happy to spell out what they think the master is getting at when he says that FDCAYF. Here's "Aaron Swords," whose Quora profile identifies him as a "computer programmer and independent conservative," rhapsodizing about the power of the mantra:

> Liberals hate this saying and shout at it with words like RACISM! and HYPOCRISY! and PRIVILEGE!
>   The thing is, when liberals shout these words with no actual evidence to back up what they are saying, it is simply proving Ben's point. Being emotional does not change the

truth about it. An example of this is gun control. It is factually proven that more gun laws take guns from legal citizens and gun free zones have the highest number of shootings in the country. However, liberals use emotional phrases like "but think about the children" instead of finding actual ways to solve the issue. Facts do not align with their emotional response.

Right now the big topic is illegal immigration. Liberals use pictures of children being separated from parents (an emotional response) to win votes. Conservatives mention that illegals are criminals and criminals are detained when they commit crimes (a factual response).

"Liberals"—a term that, in the hands of Shapiro fans, seems to refer to everyone from Nancy Pelosi through revolutionary anarcho-syndicalists—get their moral judgments from *feelings*. Steely-eyed conservatives like Ben Shapiro get *their* moral judgments from *facts*.

One way of pushing back against Mr. Swords might be to point out that some of the "facts" stated or implied here are pretty dubious. Are schools, for example, the site of more mass shootings than grocery stores because the former are "gun free zones" (and thus "soft targets" in the parlance of those who get the most excited talking about this sort of thing)? Maybe, but jumping straight to that explanation assumes that correlation implies causation. The fancy Latin name for that one is **Non Causa Pro Causa** ("Non-Cause for Cause"). More informally, it's the **Questionable Cause Fallacy**. This might seem like nitpicking. (In the 552nd installment of the webcomic XKCD, there's a painfully nerdy joke about this that always makes me laugh. The boy stick figure tells the girl stick figure that he used to believe that correlation implied causation, but he took a statistics class and now he doesn't believe that any more. The girl stick figure replies that it sounds like he learned something in the class. The boy stick figure says, "Well, maybe...") In this particular case, though, it doesn't take a lot of imagination or any particularly deep insight into the psychology of mass shooters to come up with other theories about why they might target students instead of shoppers.

Swords's flat statement that "criminals are detained" is similarly misleading. Many people who had their children separated from them at the border under Trump's policy weren't immigrants at all but asylum-seekers presenting themselves at legal ports of entry. Even if we restrict ourselves to those immigrants who "were" breaking the law, the legal facts are far more complicated than the breezy statement that "criminals are detained" would suggest. No previous administration followed Trump's 2017-2018 policy of indiscriminately criminally charging every single undocumented immigrant, and one reason why the bleeding heart liberals in, e.g. George W. Bush's administration, held back on that front is that doing so would involve mass family separation. To point this out is not to let those previous administrations off the hook for their own brutality at the border. (Anyone interested in the grisly details of the last few decades of immigration enforcement should read "The Roots of Trump's Immigration Barbarity" by Daniel Denvir and "The Democratic Precedent" by Branko Marcetic. Both appeared in *Jacobin* in the summer of 2018.) The point is that Trump's escalation of this war on undocumented immigrants was a policy choice, not something that was forced on him by any law.

The deeper problem with this "fact-based" defense of family separation is that even if there *was* some law on the books mandating that everyone picked up in the southwestern desert without legal authorization had to be criminally charged and separated from their children, this would hardly entail the conclusion in dispute between Trumpists and everyone else— that family separation was justifiable.

...and this brings us back to David Hume. Consider this argument:

Premise One: The law required the Trump Administration to separate families.
Conclusion: Separating families was the right thing to do.

The premise only supports the conclusion if we combine it with another premise, like:

Premise One: The law required the Trump Administration to separate families.
Premise Two: Obeying laws is always the right thing to do.
Conclusion: Separating families was the right thing to do.

Accepting Premise Two means, among other things, accepting that the Dutch family that sheltered Anne Frank was doing something wrong. We could try a narrower premise like:

Premise One: The law required the Trump Administration to separate families.
Premise Two*: Obeying laws enacted by democracies is always the right thing to do.
Conclusion: Separating families was the right thing to do.

Embracing Premise Two*, in turn, gets us into counterexamples about slavery and segregation. (To anticipate a very bad objection often made at this point in arguments like this one, there's a world of difference between *comparing* two injustices and saying that both would be justified by the same principle.) Perhaps there's an even narrower principle—Premise Two**— that (a) would (together with Premise One) entail the conclusion, without (b) being vulnerable to counterexamples of this type or (c) being some hopelessly *ad hoc* nonsense like, "Obeying legal requirements enacted **by the United States in the decades since the end of legal segregation** is always the right thing to do." At this point, though, it should be clear that, even if P1 were true, it wouldn't support any controversial political conclusion *on its own*.

Hume's Law (HL) generalizes this point. There are exceptions, but not interesting ones. For example, any argument with the conclusion "either abortion is wrong or it is not the case that abortion is wrong" will be technically valid, since the conclusion is a logical tautology. Remember, a valid argument is, by definition, one in which , if the premises are true, the conclusion *must* be true. Well, if the conclusion can't be false, it's not possible for the premises to all be true without the conclusion being true! Putting aside this technicality, though, the point is that the reason we *care* about whether an argument is valid or not is that in normal cases a valid argument is one where the premises (if true) give us an excellent reason to believe the conclusion. The "gold standard" of argumentation is validity—a structural guarantee that it's *impossible* to put in true premises and get out a false conclusion—but as we'll see in Chapter III many perfectly good arguments fall short of that standard. Either way, what **HL** tells us is that a purely descriptive premise (i.e. a premise about relevant nonmoral facts) can never give you a *good reason* to accept a normative conclusion (e.g. a conclusion about what someone should do, or about what actions are right or wrong or what policies are just or unjust) unless the descriptive premise is combined with an (explicit or implicit) normative premise.

I say "nonmoral facts" because philosophers love to debate about whether there are "facts" about moral rightness and wrongness or whether, for example, moral judgments are ultimately best understood as expressions of our attitudes rather than descriptions of something "out there" in the world. The first position is "moral realism" and the second is "expressivism." There are many, many other positions—so many that it would take a book longer than this one just to list them all out and summarize one or two of the standard arguments for and against them. There are also philosophers like Simon Blackburn who have interesting and complicated ways of *combining* realism and expressivism. These are deep and interesting waters, but not ones that we need to wade into right now. Whatever you make of the nature of normativity, the *logical* point is just this: To legitimately get a normative conclusion "out," you need a normative premise "in."

Of course, such premises often legitimately do go without saying. No leftist arguing that prison labor is a form of slavery feels the need to spell out the "and slavery is wrong" premise because, in the twenty-first century, not even the most dead-eyed MAGA-hat-wearing reactionary will come right out and say, "Actually, I think slavery is good!" Without the implicit "slavery is wrong" premise, though, the argument doesn't go through.

Things get more interesting when we start to think about, for example, competing notions of *freedom*. Landlords who can just sit on vast stretches of property and extract rent and business-owners who can exercise far more bargaining power than their employees in negotiations over labor contracts instinctively prioritize the kind of "freedom" that libertarians are always talking about—"freedom" defined in terms of property rights and contracts. If you're a renter and a worker, on the other hand—someone who lives under the thumbs of bosses and landlords and who has no practical choice but to do what they tell her to—you might find the more substantive notion of human freedom socialists are always talking about more appealing. This conception of freedom is all about freedom from domination—freedom to determine your own life to the extent that this is compatible with everyone else being free in the same way.

Workers taking over a factory so they can run it for themselves may or may not be doing something wrong. What you make of that issue doesn't depend *exclusively* on how good your reasoning skills are or how firmly you grasp various nonmoral facts about e.g. who holds the title to the factory. Factual premises can tell us a lot about how to achieve whatever goals we care about. They can't tell us which goals *to* care about. Centrist liberals who talk as if politics were a technocratic exercise in judging competing plans for achieving shared goals are dead wrong.

To the extent that Shapiro's point is that it's important to get the factual premises of moral and political arguments right, I agree—and I wish he would do a better job of acting on his own advice. To the extent that what he's saying is that leftists can't reason our way to our policy preferences by extrapolation from unmixed factual premises, this too is correct. To the extent, however, that his implied point is that this is a *difference* between the left and the right, he's full of shit.

III. Libertarianism and Logical Fallacies: A Guided Tour of Some Very Bad Arguments

The **composition fallacy is** the mistake we make when we jump from the premise that some part of a larger whole (or even *every* part of it) has some property, to the conclusion that the whole has it. The **division fallacy** is the equally faulty inference in the opposite direction.

Here's an example of the **composition fallacy** that you might find in a standard Critical Reasoning or Informal Logic textbook: "None of the molecules that make up the Brooklyn Bridge are visible to the naked eye, so the Brooklyn Bridge itself isn't visible to the naked eye." Flip the premise and the conclusion and you've got an instance of the **division fallacy**.

These examples vividly illustrate why arguments of this type are faulty, but not why anyone would bother learning to identify them. When it comes to such a transparently silly case, you don't have to know how to precisely classify different kinds of bad arguments to know that you're in the presence of one.

The anarchist writer Kevin Carson has pointed out a far more interesting instance of the **composition fallacy**—the one committed by apologists for capitalism who use the existence of individual upward mobility to defend structural economic inequality. To see how deep this point cuts, think about the mainstream political debate about "solutions" to poverty. Conservative rhetoric is all about individual responsibility. To the extent that liberals push back against blaming the poor for their poverty, it's because liberals emphasize *individual* obstacles to *individual* class mobility. (On this analysis, racism, bad schools, and other factors "trap" people in the lower class.) As far as it goes, the liberal objection to "individual responsibility" rhetoric is a good one. It just doesn't go very far.

What's missed in the debate between conservatives telling

burger flippers that "if you want $15 an hour, you should go back to school and get better jobs" and liberals saying "let's make college more affordable so they can do that" is that if every burger flipper got a computer programming degree, the oversupply of programmers on the labor market wouldn't magically create more programming jobs. It would just make it easy for employers to pay the programmers they *did* hire much less than they do now.

Even leftists peddling the virtues of Bernie Sanders's plan for tuition-free higher education can fall into talking as if education was a "solution" to economic inequality. Our position should be that we support universal free higher education because education is an important human good that everyone deserves access to, not because we're under the impression that if everyone went to college everyone would make more money. The way to get everyone at the bottom more money is in the short term to organize stronger labor unions and in the long term to reorganize the economic foundations of society.

Conservatives love to talk about how hard-working individuals can change class positions by starting small businesses. Liberals are more likely to talk about at least some of the obstacles that stop people from forming such businesses, and to propose a variety of schemes to make it easier for them to do so, from microloans for aspiring third world entrepreneurs to stricter enforcement of rules preventing lending discrimination against minority-owned businesses in the United States. The problem is that even when people *do* get together the starting capital to start up a small business, two thirds of such businesses fail within a decade of starting. In a competitive marketplace, the success of one business often requires the failure of another.

Taking a step back from thinking about the *specific* ways in which escape routes individuals can take to get out of poverty or even leave the working class entirely aren't available to the working class *en masse*, the more general point is a simple one:

Not every cheerleader can be on top of the pyramid. If *everyone* at the bottom of capitalism's economic hierarchy was somehow able to simultaneously move up in that hierarchy, no one would be left to harvest crops or drive food to grocery stores. We'd all starve to death. (In a socialist society, on the other hand, we could have the kind of "balanced job complexes" Michael Albert and Robin Hanhel talk about. Necessary grunt work could be spread around to allow everyone more time to do more interesting things with their lives.) The argument between liberals and conservatives about the extent to which the *premise* that "anyone" can be upwardly mobile is true serves to obscure the fallaciousness of any inference from that premise to the conclusion that large-scale economic inequality is the result of bad individual choices.

The **Equivocation Fallacy** is committed when the meaning of a term is switched in the middle of an argument to create the impression that the premises support a conclusion to which they're actually irrelevant. Here's an example I've seen used in multiple textbooks:

Premise One: Only man is rational.
Premise Two: No woman is a man.
Conclusion: No woman is rational.

This gets the idea across, and it isn't outlandishly silly like the Brooklyn Bridge illustration of the **Composition Fallacy**. The example is about something that actually matters. On the other hand, the slippage between "man" (as in humans) and "man" (as in *male* humans) is pretty blatant. A more subtle and insidious version of the **Equivocation Fallacy** is committed when conservatives and liberals argue against radical socialist experiments on the grounds that "whenever socialism has been tried before, what we've gotten have been totalitarian dictatorships." Why, such critics ask, should we believe that *this* *time* will be different?

Before addressing this argument, it's worth making explicit a distinction that I gestured at earlier in the book. Logic of any kind is the study of the connection between the premises and conclusions of arguments. Do the former support the latter? If so, how? The kind of logic we've spent most of our time on so far is *deductive* logic. This is the branch of logic that's concerned with evaluating arguments to see if they're *valid*—i.e. if the form of the argument makes it logically impossible for the premises to be true without the conclusion being true. Such an airtight connection between premises and conclusion is desirable for obvious reasons. (This is one of the reasons why philosophers have spent so much time working out the details of this kind of logic.) If you want to make sure you arrive at the truth about some subject, a deductively valid argument from premises you already know to be true is a fine thing to have. Sadly, the human epistemic condition being what it is, such arguments are in short supply. Since we have to muddle our way through the world and reason about these subjects to the best of our ability anyway, we also use *inductive* logic. This is the branch of logic where we test arguments not to see if they have valid forms but to see if they're *strong*. The deductive concept—validity—is binary. An argument can't be a little bit valid or somewhat invalid. Inductive strength, on the other hand, does come in degrees. Oftentimes, when we say that something is a "good argument," all we mean is that it's fairly strong—i.e. that the premises give us a pretty good (though far from decisive) reason to believe the conclusion.

With this distinction in our back pockets, let's go back to the Argument from Past Socialisms. At a first pass, it looks something like this:

Premise One: Past attempts to build socialism have led to horrible results.

Conclusion: If we try to build socialism in the future, this will lead to horrible results.

Our friend from the last chapter, David Hume, famously pointed out that arguments of this type—where conclusions about the future are inferred from premises about what's happened in the past—aren't valid. While the distinction between deductive and inductive logic wasn't as well understood in the eighteenth century as it is now, Hume worried that we didn't have *any* kind of rational warrant for making arguments like this. There are complex and tricky issues here, and Hume was certainly right at least that such arguments aren't *deductively* valid, but my comrades on the left shouldn't take too much solace in this verdict. As Hume himself pointed out, if we can't form expectations about the future based on the past, we wouldn't be able to navigate our way through obvious things like whether to expect the sun to rise tomorrow. Whatever one makes of Hume's "riddle" about how to make sense of this inference, it's safe to say that what's happened in the past must give us *some* reason to worry that the same thing will happen in the future.

The real problem with the argument is that, at least in so far as this argument is deployed against *democratic* socialists, who believe in political pluralism and who want an economic order based on workers' control of the means of production rather than Five-Year Plans delivered from on high by some all-powerful Central Committee, the word "socialism" doesn't mean the same thing in the premise that it means in the conclusion. Once you realize this, the Argument from Past Socialisms is no better than the argument from the unique rational capacities of the human species to the alleged cognitive superiority of male humans to female humans.

Socialists who insist that Stalinism doesn't count as "real" socialism are often accused of the **No True Scotsman** fallacy. This is a form of bad reasoning in which all evidence against a position is neutralized through *ad hoc* redefinitions of the key terms. "No Scotsman would fight a wolf outside of an elementary school." "But Groundskeeper Willie is a Scotsman, and I saw him fight a wolf outside of Springfield Elementary!" "Ah, well, if he did that, he's no *true* Scotsman!"

The problem with this accusation is that it's just not true that democratic Marxists, Chomskyite libertarian socialists, and other non-Stalinist radicals are engaging in some kind of *ad hoc* redefinition of the s-word to exclude Soviet-style states. Prior to the Russian Revolution in 1917, *everyone* used the term "socialism" to mean the extension of democracy from politics to economics. Soviet authoritarianism was vigorously denounced as early as 1918 by Rosa Luxemburg, and there's been a continuous tradition of socialists standing up against that system ever since. (That's why Michael Harrington and his comrades put that D in the name of the DSA.) Just as democratic dissidents in the Democratic People's Republic of Korea aren't playing with words when they insist that the DPRK doesn't count as a "real" democracy, socialist dissidents there aren't "redefining" anything if they insist that North Korean "socialism" is a grotesque parody of the real thing. If you make the fairly banal observation that someone born in the Canadian province of Nova Scotia ("New Scotland") doesn't count as a Scotsman, you aren't committing any sort of fallacy.

It's also worth noting that point above about how the Argument from Past Socialisms commits the **Equivocation Fallacy** stands even if we abandon — which I absolutely don't think we should — our insistence that socialism just *means* economic democracy and that Stalinism is a grotesque pseudo-socialism. Let's just call economic democracy Socialism$_1$ and Stalinism Socialism$_2$ and suspend judgment on the question of which system has a better claim to the s-word. It remains true that no premise about the failures and grotesqueries of Socialism would establish much of anything about Socialism. A really convincing argument that those failures and grotesqueries were the inevitable consequence of abandoning Free Market Principles, regardless of the direction in which they're being abandoned, would be another matter, but anyone who wants to push *that* argument has a lot more work to do than just pointing at Stalin's Russia and mocking any suggestion that "this time it will be different."

Of course, more sophisticated reactionaries often *do* claim to have such an argument. The Calculation Problem is the problem of how to line up production with consumer preferences in the absence of market mechanisms. Libertarian economic theorists like Hayek and Von Mises spilled a vast amount of ink in the Socialist Calculation Debate of the 1920s and 1930s arguing that this is an insolvable problem that dooms any attempt to go beyond capitalism to failure.

Many socialists have taken the underlying problem seriously without giving up their radical aspirations. The easiest response is to move to a "mixed" vision of socialism in which important life goods like healthcare and education are provided outside of any sort of market and the "commanding heights" of the economy are nationalized but in which a robust "private sector" of competing workers' cooperatives remains. (Bhaskar Sunkara often advocates this view in the pages of *Jacobin*. It's also one that's reflected in DSA's key strategy document, "Resistance Rising.") A much more ambitious response is the one put forward by Michael Albert and Robin Hanhel in their work on "parecon" ("participatory economics") where they outline how a decentralized, democratic, and marketless economy could coordinate production and consumption based on a complex network of workers' and consumers' councils. This proposal is vulnerable to the objection that most normal people have no interest in spending a large part of their lives in planning meetings. I've had to spend enough of mine in faculty meetings to take that objection pretty seriously. On the other hand, there's always the hope that technological advances, particularly ones related to Artificial Intelligence, might enable the automation of some of the coordinating work done by Albert and Hanhel's councils. My own suspicion is that if we're lucky enough to achieve socialism, whatever messy, historically conditioned form it ends up taking won't look exactly like any of the *a priori* blueprint radical theoreticians might draw up in the present. Those blueprints have some value, though, in showing that the Calculation Problem shouldn't be seen as some kind of decisive conversation-ending objection to socialist ideas.

A common way of expressing skepticism about any of these proposed solutions goes something like this:

"OK, fair enough, you're talking about something pretty different than the old Soviet system. But the fact remains that no successful socialist system—in your sense of 'socialism' or anyone else's—has ever existed. That's reason enough to think it's very unlikely that we can do better than capitalism."

Notice first that this is the kind of objection that can be made to *any* sort of large-scale social progress. (An example worth considering: Slavery existed in one form or another in most complex societies for most of human history.) There's also a logical problem. The objection, at least as stated, trades on treating the lack of historical evidence for the workability of economic democracy as evidence that it's *not* workable. As such, it commits the **Appeal to Ignorance** fallacy—the mistake we make when we treat the absence of evidential support for one theory as if it were evidence against it or even for some alternative view.

A much better argument in the same general neighborhood has the same premise and uses it not to conclude that we *probably* can't do better than capitalism, but that we don't really know what would happen if we, e.g. tried to translate Albert and Hanhel's scheme into reality. I think the right answer for socialists to admit is that there *are* a lot of unknowns here. The process of constructing a socialist society will involve a certain amount of trial and error, and there are real pitfalls to worry about. It's just that none of this adds up to a good enough reason to stick with the status quo. Rosa Luxemburg once wrote that humanity faced a choice between socialism and barbarism. In light of the alarming realities of profit-fueled global climate change, even "barbarism" might turn out to be optimistic.

Of course, many libertarians reject proposals to socialize the means of production not because of any such *practical* problem, or even because they believe that it will lead to somewhat more unhappiness than happiness, but because they believe that it's wrong in principle. Anyone who's argued about this stuff online is likely to have run into the view that redistributive taxation— never mind outright nationalization—is *theft* and prohibited by something called the Non-Aggression Principle (NAP). As we continue our tour of logical fallacies, it's worth lingering on the details of how exactly arguments from the NAP to anti-redistributionist conclusions are supposed to work.

Popular presentations of the NAP are often at the level of "don't initiate force against others." This makes libertarianism sound like a kind of quasi-pacifist position—pacifism with an exception built in for self-defense. Hold that thought while we consider some complications.

Imagine that you come home one day and see a robber walking away with your TV. You're outraged about theft, of course, but you aren't concerned for your safety. For one thing, he seems to be unarmed. For another, from the vantage point where you're watching him abscond with the TV, you can see him but he can't see you. If you just wait for another minute, he'll be gone. Is it morally acceptable to run after him to try to get it back?

At least in the simple form in which we've been considering the principle, the answer seems to be "no." The robber hasn't initiated force against you, but pretty much anything you do to try to get it back, from tackling him to threatening him at gunpoint, *would* count as initiating force. Even if you shout "put that down right now or I'm calling the cops," surely this is at least a threat of force—and exactly the thing you're not supposed to do except in self-defense! After all, if the robber had gotten the TV not by breaking into your house but by knocking on your door and then telling you, "Give me your TV or else I'll bring some armed men to take it from you," this would surely count as initiating force.

Any reader who actually believes in the NAP (as libertarians usually understand it) will be grumbling by now. *Of course* you can use (reasonable, proportionate) force to get your TV back! The robber started it!

The problem is that the robber didn't "start it" by using "force" against *you*, at least as "force" is usually understood. He "started it" in the sense that he entered your apartment without your permission (whether he broke a window or just realized that your door was unlocked) and taking a piece of your property. We can all agree that these are bad things to do. Even Marx and Engels explicitly say that people have a right to personal possessions, even if they don't have a right to do things like privately own factories. What, though, does this bad thing the robber is doing have to do with "initiating force"?

Here's an (apparently more precise) explanation of the NAP from libertarian writer Murray Rothbard, who is often credited with coining the phrase:

> The fundamental axiom of libertarian theory is that no one may threaten or commit violence ("aggress") against another man's person or property. Violence may be employed only against the man who commits such violence; that is, only defensively against the aggressive violence of another. In short, no violence may be employed against a non-aggressor. Here is the fundamental rule from which can be deduced the entire corpus of libertarian theory.

Notice first that the word "violence" is being used in a very

45

strange way. I know what it means to "commit violence against another man" (or woman or miniature schnauzer). What does it mean, though, to "commit violence against...his property"?

In his excellent *Current Affairs* piece "Defining Violence," Oren Nimni argues persuasively that the word "violence" is best used in a narrow and literal way. Some leftists have called everything from gentrification to cultural appropriation to charter schools "violence," but this is a mistake. We're "violent" when we physically hurt or kill people (or other beings capable of being hurt or killed). Nimni thinks that expanding the definition merely dilutes the power of the word.

He considers Rothbard's move of expanding the notion of "violence" to cover acts committed against property, but rejects it on the grounds that it entails absurd consequences. "Is it a violent act to recreationally shoot a bottle with a bb gun? To take apart an air conditioner? To eat your nachos while you aren't looking?"

How about taking that TV? Again, it's one thing to say that it's *wrong*, but is it really *violence*? Surely it isn't violence *against the TV* if the thief, wanting to use it himself, is careful not to damage it. Not having thoughts, it isn't even frightened by the experience. Still, this is precisely the sort of situation in which Rothbard's definition is supposed to authorize you to use "defensive" force. This isn't really a principle about *violence* at all, but a principle about rights—and in particular, a principle about property rights.

When we take Rothbard's definition and strip off the pseudo-pacifist rhetorical coating, we have something like this:

NAP: Do not violate someone else's rights over their person or their property unless you are doing so as part of a conflict in which the 'someone else' in question made the first move.

Before we evaluate *this* principle and the conclusions libertarians draw from it, it's worth dipping back to the Television Thief Example one more time to clarify an important distinction. Let's say the thief isn't planning to use the TV himself. Instead, he sells it to a "fence." Generally, the fence would resell it, but in this case he decides to give it away to a friend who he happens to know has a broken TV. It takes the original owner a couple days to find out what happened, but eventually he finds the TV in the apartment of the friend of the fence who bought it from the thief. Does the NAP authorize the original owner to demand it back? Does it authorize him to call the cops (or the local anarcho-capitalist militia) to help him get it back?

If the phrase "their property" in the definition of the NAP above means "property they happen to be in possession of at any given moment," then the original owner would be violating the NAP if he threatened force to get it back! Pretty clearly, what's really intended is this:

NAP: Do not violate someone else's rights over their person or their **legitimate** property unless you are doing so in a conflict where they made the first move.

...and now we run smack into a tricky problem. What makes a property claim legitimate? Note that, for libertarian claims to make any sense, this can't be a matter of *legal* legitimacy. Redistributive taxation is *legal*, and in some societies outright nationalizations are legal, but libertarians object to both. The issue is *moral* legitimacy.

Libertarian philosopher Robert Nozick argues in his book *Anarchy, State, and Utopia* that owners are morally entitled to pieces of property if they acquired them as a result of either (a) "just acts of original acquisition" or (b) legitimate transfers from someone who acquired them in one of these two ways (what Nozick cleverly calls "capitalistic acts between consenting adults"). There are several good objections to this theory. One is that it's far from obvious what makes an act of original acquisition just. If you're the first person to *see* some unclaimed piece of potential property, is it yours automatically? Do you need to occupy or use it? If you do occupy it and use it for a while and then you go away for a while, does it revert to being fair game for new acquisition? Is it yours if you just "claim" it verbally? Can you legitimately claim all the water in the world if no one else thought to do it first? Another problem is that, *however* a given libertarian works through these thorny issues, just about any halfway-plausible answer will get you the result that actually existing capitalist property relations aren't legitimate after all. After all, they didn't emerge historically from some combination of plucky citizen farmers freeholding unclaimed territory and then engaging in "capitalistic acts between consenting adults." In Europe, capitalism emerged from feudalism. In the New World, it arose through a centuries-long nightmare of slavery and genocide. Perhaps Nozick's theory could be amended to deal with this objection with some *ad hoc* emendation like "just acts of original acquisition or unjust ones for which the moral statute of limitations has elapsed," but this convoluted version would be a lot less plausible than the original principle.

There's also the question of what conditions need to apply to make the transfers legitimate. Let's take Nozick's slightly creepy analogy between sex and capitalism seriously. Person A has a large supply of food and Person B is on the brink of starvation. If A shares some of his food with B in exchange for sexual favors, how consensual is *that*? To bring things closer to a typical capitalist labor market, give Person B their choice between multiple food-hoarders—but no realistic choice except to trade sex for food with one of them. Any reasonable theory of coercion has to recognize that coerciveness comes on a spectrum, and that an arrangement can be pretty damn coercive even if all parties have given some kind of formal consent.

A further problem is that, as the great political philosopher

John Rawls pointed out, Nozick assumes that if none of the individual steps by which wealth is transferred among various participants in a market are *individually* unjust, this means that these individual steps can't add up to a cumulatively unjust distribution. That's the **Composition Fallacy.**
    With all that in mind, let's go back to the NAP.

NAP: Do not violate someone else's rights over their person or their **legitimate** property unless you are doing so in a conflict where they made the first move.

Let's pretend for a second that the economic history of the real world really happened according to a Nozickian script. The first people (maybe Adam and Eve and their descendants) slowly fanned out across the world, claiming bits of unclaimed property and consensually bartering them. By an amazing coincidence, the end result of all this was capitalism as we know it—the exact distribution of wealth and ownership that exists in the real world. A social democratic government in this world imposes high taxes on the rich to pay for social programs to secure what it regards as social rights to healthcare and higher education. Has the NAP been violated? Or even—a radical socialist movement in this hypothetical world succeeds in overthrowing the existing economic order entirely in favor of a new system based on collective ownership and workplace democracy. Has the NAP been violated?
    Well, it has *if* Nozick's theory of morally legitimate property is the right one. On the other hand, if the right theory of distributive justice is an egalitarian one, according to which everyone is entitled to the same standard of living, then *the NAP has not been violated*. If some third theory is the right one....then maybe the NAP has been violated and maybe it hasn't, depending on the details of that third theory. The NAP just tells you not to violate morally legitimate property claims. It doesn't tell you—

it *can't* tell you—which property claims are morally legitimate. Here's Matt Bruenig of the People's Policy Project, spelling out what that means about arguments from the NAP for libertarian economic conclusions:

> Suppose I go to tax you. My claim is simple. You are not, under my theory of distributive justice, entitled to the amount I am taxing you. It does not belong to you. It belongs to the retired person it is headed to. You then resist. So I use force where necessary to extract the tax.
>
> Now there are two moves you can make here, one makes sense and the other doesn't. The one that makes sense is to say: this is an unjust tax because the amount being taxed belongs to me, and I am entitled to it. The one that doesn't make sense and does no argumentative work whatsoever is to say: this is aggression.
>
> The reason it makes no sense is because it does what philosophers call *begging the question*. Why is taxing you aggression rather than defense? Well it's aggression because you are entitled to what is being taxed from you (you claim). Fine, I hear that you believe it belongs to you. But I don't believe it belongs to you. So really when you say it is aggression, you are just assuming as an unstated premise exactly what we are disagreeing about: whether the thing actually belongs to you or not. If I am right about the thing not belonging to you, it's not aggression. If you are right about it belonging to you, it is.
>
> So calling it aggression when we are disputing whether it belongs to you literally does nothing in the debate. You've just restated that you think the thing belongs to you with different words. You didn't do any argumentative work.

One interesting thing about the **Begging the Question** (*Petitio Principii*) fallacy is that question-begging arguments are deductively valid arguments. If you smuggle the conclusion into the premises, then by definition if the premises are true, the conclusion will be true too. Nonetheless, question-begging arguments are clearly *bad* arguments.

Think about Fermat's Last Theorem. (This example is a modified version of one used by Edwin Mares in his book on "relevance logic.") The theorem states that no three positive integers a, b, and c satisfy the equation $a^n + b^n = c^n$ for any value of n greater than 2. The seventeenth century mathematician Pierre de Fermat famously scribbled this in the margins of a book — and a note claiming that he had a simple and elegant proof that was too large to fit in those margins. No one knows what Fermat's proof was (if he really had one), but the British mathematician Andrew Wiles successfully offered a proof in the 1990s. He announced it in 1993 at a talk in Cambridge, but an error was discovered a few months later. In 1994, he found a way to correct the error, and in 1995 he published the corrected version to great acclaim. He received various honors and awards. He was *knighted*. It was a big deal.

Imagine, however, that Wiles had saved the seven years of research time it took him to come up with the actual proof, and instead he'd gone up to that podium at Cambridge and presented the following simple proof, which it took me two seconds to come up with:

Premise One: No three integers a, b, and c will satisfy the equation $a^n + b^n = c^n$ for any value of n greater than 2.

Conclusion. No three integers a, b, and c will satisfy the equation $a^n + b^n = c^n$ for any value of n greater than 2.

It's a deductively valid argument. If the premise is true, so is the conclusion! Even so, if Wiles had presented my proof instead of his, he wouldn't have been knighted.

Usually, question-begging arguments don't wear their question-beggingness on their sleeve the way my proof of Fermat's Last Theorem does. Most of the ones you encounter "in the wild" (outside of toy examples you encounter in books about logic) are more like the argument against taxation "from the NAP." Or like the reasoning of the anti-abortion protester who says she's against abortion *because it's murder.* The concept of wrongness is already baked into the concept of murder. The reason we don't talk about, for example, "murdering attackers in self-defense" is that part of what we mean when we call a killing murder is that it's morally unjustified. So "abortion is wrong because it's murder" reduces to "abortion is wrong because it's wrong."

Not to let the left off the hook here, I've heard the "because it's murder" non-argument used to object to both the death penalty and the slaughter of animals for human consumption. Whatever one thinks about either vegetarianism or death penalty abolitionism, we should all be able to agree that these are terrible arguments.

Begging the Question is bad because the purpose of an argument is to give the listener or reader who doesn't already accept the conclusion a reason to change her mind. Someone who doesn't already believe that abortion is wrong or that $a^n + b^n = c^n$ doesn't hold for values of n greater than 2 isn't given any reason to *start* believing it by a question-begging argument.

Logic nerds often grumble about the way the phrase "begging the question" is popularly used to mean *raising* the question. I know I do. The mistake in reasoning we make when we (knowingly or unknowingly) treat the conclusions we're arguing for as *reasons to believe* those conclusions is a common and important one. We need a term for it—and good luck getting everyone to say **Petitio Principii** instead. When pundits say things like, "the nominee evaded the question twelve times in the hearing, which begs the question, what is he hiding," they could just as easily say "which *raises* the question." Saying it that way would only add one lousy syllable.

That said, I wouldn't deny that a certain kind of logic nerd gets entirely *too* worked up about this bit of semantic drift. Making a big deal out of correcting people for misusing the phrase is a way of performing just how much you know about this stuff. As such, it's precisely the sort of behavior you can expect from the kind of right-wing "logicbros" discussed in Chapter I— the kind who love to barrage people with the names of logical fallacies in social media debates. Well, a lot of those people are libertarians who think that nationalizations (and even taxpayer-funded social programs) violate the NAP. That's why Bruenig's argument is a thing of beauty. When you're arguing about the ethics of nationalizations (or even just redistributive taxation) with one of them, you can wait while they accuse you of every logical fallacy they've ever heard of and then calmly explain that the argument they appealed to five minutes ago *actually* begs the question.

IV. A is A: Ayn Rand, Leon Trotsky, and What Logic *Isn't*

Here's the sort of example you're likely to encounter in the first chapter of an introductory symbolic logic textbook:

Premise One: Either John is at home or he is at the library.
Premise Two: John is not at home.
Conclusion: John is at the library.

Here's a somewhat more interesting argument with the same logical structure:

Premise One: Either social democratic reforms will be sufficient to solve the problems of capitalism or those problems can only be solved by expropriating the means of production.
Premise Two: Social democratic reforms will not be sufficient to solve the problems of capitalism.

Conclusion: Those problems can only be solved by expropriating the means of production.

The common structure (called "Disjunctive Syllogism") is:
Premise One: Either P or Q
Premise Two: Not-P
Conclusion: Q

To represent this in the language of symbolic logic, we symbolize the "either...or" with the disjunction symbol "∨" and the "not" with the negation symbol "¬." The Ps and Qs are just variables that can represent any statement, the way the xs and ys in algebra can stand for any number. The symbols are "logical constants," and they can be defined precisely with what logicians call "truth tables." A truth table is a way of visualizing all the possible ways that a certain kind of statement can be true or false. Here's the truth table for negation:

¬P
FT
TF

If the original statement P is true, the negated statement "not-P" is false and we write an "F" under the negation symbol. (If "snow is white" is true, "snow is not white" is false.) If P is false, "not-P" is true. (If "snow is green" is false, "snow is not green" is true.) Pretty simple.

Here's the one for disjunction:

P ∨ Q
T T T
T T F
F T T
F F F

Here's how to read this:

Each horizontal line represents one possible combination of P standing for something true, P standing for something false, Q standing for something true, or Q standing for something false. The truth value of the whole statement "Either P or Q" is written under the disjunction symbol in the middle. So, for example, on the two middle lines, one of the two disjuncts (i.e. one of the two things being "or"-ed) is true and the other is false, so the whole disjunction comes out as true and a little "T" is written under the disjunction symbol. (Think, "Either a Republican will win the 2020 election or a Democrat will win the 2020 election." That's almost certainly true, because even though one of the two disjuncts is false—we don't know which one yet—the other will almost certainly be true.) The only line where the disjunction comes out false and a little "F" is written under the disjunction symbol is the line where "P" and "Q" are both false. (Think, "Either a Green Party candidate or a Libertarian Party candidate will win the 2020 election.") But what about the top line?

Well, the "either...or" of ordinary English is ambiguous. Some disjunctions are inclusive ("P or Q or both") and some are exclusive ("P or Q but not both"). The "∨" symbolizes inclusive disjunction, which is why the first line of the truth table above comes out as "true." If you want to express the exclusive kind of disjunction in the language of symbolic logic, you write "(P ∨ Q) ∧ ¬(P ∧ Q)." As you might guess, "∧" is the conjunction symbol— "P ∧ Q" is just "P and Q." This is the truth table for conjunction:

P ∧ Q
T T T
T F F
F F T
F F F

Once we have this symbolic language in place, we can use it to evaluate whole argument forms to see if they're valid or invalid. Remember from the discussion earlier in the book that an argument is valid if its structure makes it logically impossible for the premises to all be true without the conclusion being true as well. Since a truth table is just a representation of all the logical possibilities, with each horizontal line representing one possible combination of truth and falsity, we can just test whether an argument is valid or invalid by seeing if there are any lines where the premises all come out "T" and the conclusion comes out "F." (Remember, the single / means what's coming next is another premise and the double // means what's coming next is the conclusion.) Here's the table for Disjunctive Syllogism:

P ∨ Q / ¬P // Q
T T T   FT   T
T T F   FT   F

```
F T T  TF   T
F F F  TF   F
```

Scanning the truth table, we see that "P ∨ Q" and "¬P" are only both true in one place—the third line down. Since the conclusion "Q" also comes out as true on that line, the argument's valid. (There's no possible combination of Ts and Fs that makes all the premises true and the conclusion false.) On the other hand, consider this argument:

Premise One: Either political freedom is important or economic equality is important.

Premise Two: Political freedom is important.

Conclusion: Economic equality is not important.

The first premise can be read as an exclusive disjunction or an inclusive one. If it's exclusive—that is to say, if the logical form of the premise is $(P \lor Q) \land \neg(P \land Q)$—then it's a bad argument for the simple reason that, at least if it's supposed to be an argument against *democratic* socialism, it starts by assuming what needs to be proved—that we can't have *both* freedom and equality. (See our discussion of **Begging the Question** in Chapter III.) On the other possible interpretation—that the disjunction is inclusive— then this argument form (the **Fallacy of Asserting a Disjunct**) is invalid. To see why, look at its truth table:

```
P ∨ Q / P // ¬Q
T T T  T   FT
T T F  T   TF
F T T  F   FT
F F F  F   TF
```

On the very first line, "P ∨ Q" is true, "P" is true," and "¬Q" is false.

...and right around this point, depending on your temperament, you might be wondering if this is all just a massive waste of time. The idea that we really need such elaborate logical machinery to know that the argument just given is a bad one might seem like the philosophical equivalent of thinking that we need to analyze an insect down to the molecular level before we swat it.

A three-level response is appropriate here. First, when we strip our reasoning processes down to the bone to see *exactly* how they work (and where they can go wrong), we're expanding human knowledge in an interesting way. Let's not be like the neoliberal corporatists in university administrations who demand that every line of inquiry justify itself in "practical" and not just human terms. Second, the part about "how arguments can go wrong" actually does have concrete consequences. We saw quite a bit of that in Chapter III. Granted, that discussion mostly revolved around *informal* logical fallacies, but the point holds even when it comes to the more formal parts of logic. Just as advertisers and politicians can trick a mathematically illiterate populace with misleading claims about statistics, a huckster like Ben Shapiro can make an invalid mess of an argument and leave people nodding along because they're responding to the fast, loud, and confident way that he talks rather than attending to the faulty structure of the arguments themselves.

Before we get to the third point, though, notice that the logical machinery explored above rests on two fundamental principles, the **Law of the Excluded Middle** and the **Law of Non-Contradiction.**

- **Law of the Excluded Middle (LEM):** Every statement is either true or false.
- **Law of Non-Contradiction (LNC):** No statement is both true and false.

The **LEM** tells us that the logical possibilities are restricted to T and F, the **LNC** that truth tables shouldn't include any lines in which a statement comes out as *both* T and F. A narrower corollary of the **LNC is** the **Law of Identity**.

- **Law of Identity (LI):** Nothing can fail to be identical to itself.

Oddly enough, it's at *this* point, just when the sense that this is all a giant exercise in spelling out obvious things in unnecessary detail might become overwhelming, that things become philosophically and politically controversial. The acolytes of Russian-American novelist and "objectivist" guru Ayn Rand often seem to suggest that the three principles just mentioned somehow add up to the basis of an argument for Rand's moral and political ideas. *A is A*—therefore, everyone should support free market capitalism!

Rand was twelve when her countrymen overthrew first the Tsar and then the Provisional Government. Viscerally disgusted by the new Communist system, she left for the United States as soon as she'd graduated from college. In several works of "literature" where the good guys can be differentiated from the bad guys by whether they agree with the philosophical and political opinions of the author, she preached a worldview that stood the Bolshevism she'd fled from on its head. Marxists argue that the working class has the power to change society because workers can withhold their labor and grind everything around them to a halt. Rand inverts this in her 1957 novel *Atlas Shrugged*, in which hero John Galt leads the captains of industry to "Galt's Gulch," where they withdraw from society until the left-wing government collapses and everyone realizes how indispensable they are.

Why, one might wonder, wouldn't the left-wing government just nationalize these people's businesses? Alternately, why wouldn't their employees reopen the abandoned enterprises as workers' cooperatives—like their real life counterparts have done in a variety of situations ranging from the Paris Commune to Argentina's "retaken factories" movement? If they had, they could do just fine without the bosses in the Gulch. A whole body of research shows that such cooperatives are actually *more* productive than traditional capitalist businesses.

To make her scenario even slightly plausible, Rand needs low-level engineering whizzes and the "creative minds" in the R&D departments to side with the "business leaders" and accompany them to Galt's Gulch...unlike the real life engineers in, for example, Henry Ford's Detroit, who joined the UAW. Without this assumption in place, the story would have ended with the captains of industry starving to death and their skeletons being discovered decades later when hardy socialist mountain-climbers happen to stumble upon Galt's Gulch.

All in all, *Atlas Shrugged* might sound like a fairly juvenile exercise in political wish fulfillment. Rand and her followers, however, see it as an expression of her deep commitment to Reason. The three sections of the novel are entitled "Non-Contradiction," "Either-Or," and "A is A."

How exactly are these basic logical axioms supposed to lend any kind of support to Rand's extremely specific moral and economic and political conclusions? One might not expect anyone but her most devoted followers to take seriously the idea that they do, but at least a few of her left-wing interlocutors seem to be strangely willing to concede the point. In a review of Rand's posthumously published novel *Ideal* in *The New Republic,* Catholic socialist Elizabeth Bruenig says that Rand's devotees called her "Mrs. Logic." Bruenig concedes that Rand "may have been wedded to a kind of reason," but opines that "she failed to recognize it as only one kind, and understood all others—the logic of love, the sense of beauty, the intuition of kindness—only in a mirror, very darkly."

Bruenig comes uncomfortably close here to just conceding the "kind of reason" that actually involves *reasoning* to reactionaries like Rand, instead reserving for the left the "kind of reason" that boils down to intensely feeling noble emotions about love and beauty and kindness. This strikes me as a strange and totally unnecessary gift to the other side. Why not instead demand, as a math teacher might put it, to see Rand's work? Just *how* do Non-Contradiction and the Excluded Middle and the rest enter into the debate about whether self-sacrificing altruism is better or worse than Rand's moral individualism? (No, don't give me stirring rhetoric *about* Reason. Actually show me some reasoning! Preferably with numbered lists of premises and clearly identified inferential steps.) Is it really plausible that the debate between the radical left and apologists for capitalism hinges on the question of whether A occasionally fails to be A... or is it vastly more likely that the two camps are separated by a divergence in substantive premises about history and morality and economic theory?

To ask this question, one might think, is to answer it. Oddly enough, at least one historically important socialist seems to have agreed with Rand that the "A is A" issue is relevant to the dispute after all. Leon Trotsky, one of the key leaders of the revolution that so horrified the young Ayn Rand, wrote about this subject in almost the same way that Rand did—but with the pluses and minuses reversed. Standard logic is wrong and it leads to incorrect political conclusions!

Here's John Galt in his big speech in *Atlas Shrugged*:

Whatever you choose to consider, be it an object, an attribute, or an action, the law of identity remains the same. A leaf cannot be a stone at the same time, it cannot be all red and green at the same time, it cannot freeze and burn at the same time... Are you seeking to know what is wrong with the world? All the disasters that have wrecked your world, came from your leaders' attempt to evade the fact that A is A. All the secret evil you dread to face within you and all the pain you have ever endured, came from your own attempt to evade the fact that A is A. The purpose of those who taught you to evade it was to make you forget that Man is Man.

Here's Trotsky in his 1939 article *A Petty-Bourgeois Opposition in the Socialist Workers Party*:

> The Aristotelian logic of the simple syllogism starts from the proposition that "A" is equal to "A." ...But in reality "A" is not equal to "A." This is easy to prove if we observe these two letters under a lens – they are quite different from each other. But, one can object, the question is not of the size or the form of the letters, since they are only symbols for equal quantities, for instance, a pound of sugar. The objection is beside the point; in reality a pound of sugar is never equal to a pound of sugar – a more delicate scale always discloses a difference. Again one can object: but a pound of sugar is equal to itself. Neither is this true – all bodies change uninterruptedly in size, weight, color, etc. They are never equal to themselves...

The fundamental flaw of vulgar thought lies in the fact that it wishes to content itself with motionless imprints of a reality which consists of eternal motion. Dialectical thinking gives to concepts, by means of closer approximations, corrections, concretizations, a richness of content and flexibility; I would even say a succulence which to a certain extent brings them close to living phenomena. Not capitalism in general, but a given capitalism at a given stage of development. Not a workers' state in general, but a given workers' state in a backward country in an imperialist encirclement, etc.

Trotsky is always a clear and forceful writer, and he's often an insightful thinker, but this is far from his best work. Like Rand, he seems confused about the import of the **LI**. Even theorists who categorically deny that humans have *any* sort of fixed psychological or moral nature can and should cheerfully acknowledge that Man is Man. This declaration will be equivalent from their perspective to the singularly uninteresting observation that "humans (a species without any sort of fixed psychological or moral nature)" are "humans (a species without any sort of fixed psychological or moral nature)."

The **LI** tells us that whatever objects may exist are by definition identical to themselves. Whether those objects change from one moment to the next or stay the same over time is an entirely separate question. As we learn from observation (rather than from any sort of direct inference from the laws of logic), objects *do* change over time in all sorts of interesting ways. Still, far from the fact of constant change somehow undermining the logical tautology that everything is identical to itself, the former would be inexplicable without the latter. Let A be Trotsky's slowly leaking bag of sugar—the one whose weight at any given moment only approximates a pound. It can only be true that the precise amount of sugar in A *changed* between Time T1 and Time T2 if the same bag existed at both times. Otherwise, we simply have a bag of sugar with one weight at T1 and a bag with another bag at T2, not a single changing bag.

To be fair, Trotsky anticipates this objection.

A sophist will respond that a pound of sugar is equal to itself "at any given moment." Aside from the extremely dubious practical value of this "axiom," it does not withstand theoretical criticism either. How should we really conceive the word "moment"? If it is an infinitesimal interval of time, then a pound of sugar is subjected during the course of that "moment" to inevitable changes. Or is the "moment" a purely mathematical abstraction, that is, a zero of time? But everything exists in time; and existence itself is an uninterrupted process of transformation; time is consequently a fundamental element of existence. Thus the axiom "A" is equal to "A" signifies that a thing is equal to itself if it does not change, that is, if it does not exist.

This response falls flat for at least two reasons. The first is that Trotsky probably got the physics wrong. The second and more important reason is that even if he was right about the scientific issue, it would be irrelevant to the underlying point about *logic*.

As far back as 1899, the physicist Max Planck proposed that the smallest unit of time in principle was 5.39×10^{-44} seconds. Since ".39×10^{-44} seconds" doesn't exactly roll off the tongue, contemporary physicists generally refer to this as "a Planck interval." The issue is a tricky one, since it involves complex questions about the difficulties involved in fitting the results of quantum and relativistic physics into a single coherent picture, so even now no consensus among physicists about whether Planck-sized moments of time really are indivisible into smaller units. Still, it's a bad idea for Marxists to get into the habit of rejecting scientific results—even controversial ones—because they sound "undialectical." Anyone who needs convincing on this point is advised to Google the history of "Lysenkoism" in the Soviet Union.

More importantly, whoever's right about the nature of time, and no matter how intrinsically interesting that discussion may be, it has absolutely nothing to do with the **LI**. The laws of logic can tell us that "A (a bag of sugar whose weight hovers right around a pound over the course of an arbitrarily short interval of time)" can never fail to be identical to "A (a bag of sugar whose weight hovers right around a pound over the course of an arbitrarily short amount of time)." Logic itself, unaided by empirical data, can't tell us a damned thing about whether bags of sugar with precise weights exist at precise moments of time.

This is all so straightforward that a reader sympathetic to Trotsky might suspect that some subtler point is being missed.

Perhaps his real objection is not just to the **LI** but to the whole "Aristotelian" framework of the **LEM** and the **LNC**. His line of thought could be something like this: If a properly dialectical thinker wants to theorize about all the nuanced details of the dynamics of "a given capitalism at a given state of development," then statements that capitalism *is* like this or *isn't* like that won't fit into the simple categories of "true (but not false)" and "false (but not true)." Maybe his idea is that the complexity of the subject matter demands classifying some such statements as *both* true and false or *neither* true nor false.

If this was his point, it's exactly wrong. Just as logical rigor is valuable because it forces us to be *consistent*, it's valuable because it forces us to be *clear*. In casual conversation, we often use superficially inconsistent language as a way of gesturing at complexity. "How did the job interview go?" "Well, it was good and it wasn't." We might do the same thing in similarly brief discussions of more theoretical subjects. "Is it true that capitalism is dynamic?" "Well, it's sort of true." Clarifying a complex idea to show that and how it's internally consistent requires spelling it out in all its dialectical nuance. "Here's the specific way in which capitalism is dynamic. Here's the entirely compatible subtle respect in which it's undynamic."

Trotsky's essay was written in the context of a debate about the "given workers' state in a backward country" alluded to above. Stalin's Russia had just signed a diplomatic pact with Hitler's Germany. This development rocked the international communist movement. Until then, the Struggle Against Fascism was a defining element of the politics of the world's capital-C Communist Parties. It would become one again in two years, when Hitler broke the treaty and invaded the Soviet Union. For the moment, though, the fascists were partners in Comrade Stalin's Wise Peace Policy. All around the world, fiercely committed communists left the movement in disgust, driven by the same kind of conflict between socialist values and ugly

Stalinist realities that would drive later waves of defections from the world's Communist Parties when, for example, Soviet tanks rolled into Budapest in 1956 and Prague in 1968.

In principle, the crisis for capital-C Communism should have been an opportunity for the small-c communists of Trotsky's Fourth International. *Disgusted by the hypocrisies of Stalinism? Well, comrades, come join us!* But, as it happened, the Molotov-Ribbentrop Pact created a small crisis even within Trotsky's movement. Ever since Stalin consolidated power and wiped out the last traces of workers' democracy in the early Soviet Union, Trotsky's analysis had been that for all its decay the USSR was still a semi-socialist configuration—a "degenerated workers' state" in Trotsky's parlance—that could in principle be restored to its former glory. Continuing to accept the "workers' state" analysis as Hitler and Stalin divided up Poland between them meant thinking that the invading army imposing the Soviet system on unwilling Poles—in cooperation with the Nazi forces assimilating the other half of the country into the Third Reich—were "objectively" empowering the Polish working class. For a dissident faction in the Socialist Workers Party, the American affiliate of Trotsky's Fourth International, this was too much to swallow. Max Schactman and his co-thinker James Burnham moved toward an analysis of the Soviet order as a non-capitalist but thoroughly non-socialist system of "bureaucratic collectivism"—less like a "workers' state," as Schactman liked to say, than a "workers' prison."

So what does any of this have to do with logical truisms like the **LEM**, the **LNC**, and the **LI**? Nothing…except that in the subsequent debate Trotsky leaned hard on talk of "dialectics" and "dialectical logic" and accusations that the analysis being offered by the opposition faction was "undialectical." Burnham, a philosophy professor at NYU who was at least somewhat aware of the kind of formal symbolic logic being developed by contemporaries like Bertrand Russell and Jan Lukasiewicz, responded that logic had progressed quite a bit since the nineteenth century and that the sort of "dialectical logic" Hegel and Marx had talked about was no longer relevant.

At this point, horrified by Burnham's apparent deviation from Marxist orthodoxy, Trotsky and his American lackey James P. Cannon started talking non-stop not about the economic nature of the Soviet Union but about *logic*. "Marxism without the dialectic," Trotsky said, "is like a clock without a spring." Clearly, the opposition was coming to the wrong conclusions about the USSR because they were using the wrong logical methodology.

When Burnham resigned from the SWP and moved to the right, this was taken as instant confirmation of this diagnosis. When Max Schactman, decades later, gave up his radical political positions, later Trotskyists took this as a belated confirmation of everything the Old Man had said about dialectics and the rest.... despite several obvious problems with this analysis.

For one thing, Schactman didn't actually share Burnham's reservations about the dialectical method. Trotskyists who take this history as a morality tale about the dangers of abandoning orthodox Marxism tend to gloss over this point and insist that Schactman was somehow tainted with Burnham's un-dialectical-ness.

Second, Burnham and Schactman's political journeys were strikingly different. Disillusioned by his falling out with Trotsky, Burnham simply dropped his socialist politics in 1940. Schactman stuck to his guns. When the faction fight within the SWP came to a head and Schactman left to form the rival Workers Party, he took many of the SWP's best trade unionists with him. The Workers' Party spent the 1940s inciting wildcat strikes on factory floors and talking as if an American socialist revolution might be right around the corner. Over the course of the ensuing decades, he gradually abandoned these hopes. By the mid-1960s, he'd softened into a fairly moderate social democrat and, crucially, he'd abandoned his radical critique of American foreign policy. In particular, concurring with the shameful position of many of the moderate labor leaders with which he now associated, he supported American involvement in Vietnam. One doesn't have to make any excuses for this political degeneration to be unpersuaded that its causes could be traced back to flaws in the positions he took in one particular faction fight decades earlier.

This brings us to a third and deeper problem with the standard Trotskyist take on this history. This analysis is a textbook example of (and a perfect example of what's wrong with) the **Post Hoc Ergo Propter Hoc** fallacy. ("After it, therefore because of it.") Legions of radicals from the 1930s generation had moved to the right by the time Nixon-inspired hardhats were beating up anti-war protesters in the late 1960s. Some, like Burnham, had Road to Damascus moments while the class struggle was still burning white hot. Many others, like Schactman, drifted toward more moderate political positions during the long postwar boom. The ranks of the formerly radical included not only ex-Schactmanites, but plenty of ex-Trotskyists who'd sided with Trotsky and Cannon against Schactman and Burnham in the 1939 faction fight, and for that matter plenty of ex-leftists whose journey went straight from the Communist Party to the political mainstream without a detour through Trotskyism. Nor did everyone who was on Burnham and Schactman's side in 1939, or who associated with Schactman after the split, eventually drift to the right. Major organizations on the contemporary left, like Solidarity and the International Socialist Organization, can trace their political lineage back to "Schactmanites" like Hal Draper who stayed true to their principles. The main founder of the DSA, Michael Harrington, was influenced by the later Schactman in many ways—some good and some bad—but he had better positions on a variety of issues, including the war in Vietnam. In light of all this, even if Schactman *had* shared Burnham's hostility to "dialectical logic" in 1939, why should we believe that this was the crucial step away from the path of political righteousness that led him to support American imperialism decades later? A Stalinist arguing that Schactman's crucial deviation had been supporting Trotsky against Stalin in the late 1920s would be making a bad and silly argument, but not a particularly worse or sillier argument than the ones generally made on this point by orthodox Trotskyists.

Finally, and most importantly, the set of analytical principles sometimes called "dialectical logic" (or, more helpfully, "the dialectical method") have almost nothing to do with "logic" in the sense that the term is used in this book. The latter is about analyzing *arguments*, the former about analyzing social forces and situations. Some of the same words, like "contradiction," are used in both contexts, but they're used in completely different ways. A logical "contradiction" is committed when a statement and its negation are simultaneously asserted. This is pretty obviously not what's going on when Marx and Engels speak, for example, about the "contradiction" between the proletariat and the bourgeoisie.

The best analysis I've seen of the relationship between the two kinds of "logic" comes from Chris Matthew Sciabarra's book *Ayn Rand: Russian Radical*. He quotes Rand's characterization of Marx's philosophy of dialectical materialism as the view "that *contradictions* are the law of reality, that is A is non-A." Sciabarra is far more sympathetic to his subject than I am, but he knows the history of philosophy well enough to push back against her view on this point.

More than two thousand years after Aristotle's death, Hegel developed a conception of dialectics as an ontological and historical process. Hegel's dialectical method affirms the impossibility of logical contradiction, while focusing instead on *relational* 'contradictions' or paradoxes revealed in the dynamism of history... 'Dialectical materialists' placed this process on an economic foundation, and used it as the basis for a philosophy of history.

A relational "contradiction" is a dynamic tension between two elements of a larger system. The dialectical method is a way of analyzing social forces that closely attends to relational contradictions in order to see possibilities for conflict and change that might not show up in a more static analysis of things as they are at a given moment.

This method is a good one. Trotsky is right to say that we should investigate the nuances of "a given capitalism at a given state of development" and not just rely on theoretical abstractions about "capitalism in general." Happily, we don't have to choose between taking his advice and caring about logical consistency.

Sadly, Chris Sciabarra wasn't around in 1939 to explain all this to Burnham and Trotsky. If he had been, they might have realized that they were talking past each other in the argument about "logic." Once that was cleared up, everyone involved could have gotten back to arguing about Russia.

V. Technocratic Centrism and Inductive Logic: A Note on Nate Silver

The fallacies we looked at in Chapter III were "informal fallacies"—ways in which the premises of an argument can fail to provide support for the conclusion because of their *content*. The **Composition** and **Division** fallacies, for example, trade on the arbitrary assumption that the properties of parts will line up with the properties of the larger wholes composed by those parts. In Chapters I and IV, we also looked at a couple of formal fallacies, like **Asserting the Consequent** and **Asserting a Disjunct**. These are ways that reasoning can go wrong because of the *logical form* of arguments—ways that arguments can look deductively valid while actually being invalid.

In between informal fallacies and formal *deductive* fallacies there are probabilistic fallacies—ways that an argument can misleadingly seem to be inductively strong. Remember from Chapter III that a strong inductive argument is one where the truth of the premises would make it very likely (though not certain) that the conclusion is true.

A straightforward probabilistic fallacy is the **Gambler's Fallacy**. You've flipped a coin nine times and it's come up tails every time, so you think heads is "due." What are the chances that it would come up tails *ten times*?

Well, as a matter of fact, if we assume that it's a fair coin (so the chance of *any individual flip* coming up tails is exactly .5) the chance of a string of ten flips in a row coming up tails:

T T T T T T T T T T

...is .5 x .5 x .5 x .5 x. 5 x .5 x .5 x .5 x .5 x. 5, which works out to 1/1,024 (or about .000967). That's not very much. On the other hand, the chances of nine flips coming up tails and then one coming up heads:

T T T T T T T T H

...is exactly the same 1/1,024. So is the chance of a less surprising string like:

T H T H H T H T T H

...because *any* string of any combination of heads and tails is exactly as likely as any other string given a fair coin. The reason is that the probability of each flip is independent. The probability of *this particular* toss of a fair coin coming up heads given that it came up tails nine times before is .5, just like the probability of the first flip coming up tails....because the "given that" is irrelevant. The coin doesn't remember the previous flips.

A slight variation on the **Gambler's Fallacy** is the **Hot Hands** fallacy. The coin has come up tails nine times before, so tails is clearly on a roll and it's more likely that the next flip will come up tails than heads. The mathematical problem here is exactly the same.

A slightly more interesting probabilistic fallacy is the **Conjunction Fallacy**. The classic illustration, due to Aaron Tversky and Daniel Kahneman, is about a character named Linda.

Linda is 31 years old, single, outspoken, and very bright. She majored in philosophy. As a student, she was deeply concerned with issues of discrimination and social justice, and also participated in anti-nuclear demonstrations. Which is more probable?

1. Linda is a bank teller.

2. Linda is a bank teller and is active in the feminist

movement.

In Tversky and Kahneman's study, more than 80% of participants chose 2. Even people who know enough about statistics to know better often choose 2, since it just feels *obvious*. The problem is that, in any case where two statements A and B *can* come apart— one can be true without the other being true—the probability of just one of those statements being true is always greater than the probability that both are true.

Let $P(A)$ be the probability that Linda is a bank teller and $P(B)$ be the probability that Linda is an active feminist. It's certainly true that the information we've been given about Linda gives us more reason to suspect that she's an active feminist than that she's a bank teller. To see why that doesn't matter, think of it like this: Probabilities are like slices of the pie of possibilities. Whatever the size of the $P(A)$ slice, it's true just as a matter of logic that this slice can be divided into two smaller slices—the probability that Linda is a bank teller *and an active feminist* [$P(A \land B)$] and the probability that Linda is a bank teller *and not an active feminist* [$P(A \land \neg B)$]. Even if $P(A \land \neg B)$ is, on its own, only a tiny slice of pie—much smaller than the $P(A \land B)$ slice—it remains true that the two slices put together take up more of the piece than either of the slices on its own.

A probabilistic fallacy that's much easier to wrap your head around is the fallacy of **Hasty Generalization**. A statistical generalization is an argument from facts about some random sample of a larger population to a conclusion about the larger population. If pollsters want to know how many Americans are planning to vote to re-elect Donald Trump, they can't realistically ask all two hundred and thirty five million eligible voters—or even the hundred million of them who are most likely to actually bother to vote. If you poll 10,000 likely voters—.0001% of them— that's an *amazing* sample.

On the other hand, if I do a poll of my socialist and communist friends, and I get the result that 0% of likely voters are planning to vote to re-elect the President...that's worthless, because I've committed the **Hasty Generalization** fallacy. I've come to a conclusion about the larger population from a sample that isn't large enough or randomized enough to be meaningful.

Hold that thought while we talk about my high school classmate Nate Silver.

I was a Freshman at East Lansing High School in 1994. Nate was already a Junior, but we knew each other slightly because we were both on the debate team. (Yes, yes, I can hear those of you with Felix Biederman-like opinions about logic nerds snickering at this piece of information. Let's move on.) We weren't friends, but we were friendly acquaintances. I went to his house once to prepare for a debate meet. I remember that his family was nice, and that they had a three-legged dog. That's about it. When he rose to prominence many years later, as a poll-cruncher in the 2008 and 2012 elections, I was vaguely tickled by it, the way you are if someone you used to know a little gets a pro-football contract or lands a role on a hit TV show.

There were always signs that Nate's political judgment was Not Great. His 2012 book *The Signal and the Noise,* for example, includes a fawning interview with war criminal Colin Powell.

In 2013, French economist Thomas Piketty wrote a much better book called *Capital in the Twenty-First Century.* Wading through an enormous amount of data on the distribution of wealth in Europe and the United States over the course of centuries, Piketty documented a trend toward extreme inequality rooted in the intergenerational accumulation of wealth by those at the top of society. Piketty's book was a surprise bestseller—at least, I don't know anyone who would have predicted that an eight hundred-page tome by a French economist would be a bestseller in the United States—and it helped focus attention on economic inequality.

Nate's commentary on Piketty at his venue 538 was almost a

caricature of what a smug liberal technocrat might say. He tried to sagely split the difference between Piketty and his right-wing critics at *The Economist* and did so in a way that ignored a lot of what Piketty had already written in reply to those critics. Worse yet, he started his post with this "series of disclosures":

> First, my economic priors and preferences are closer to *The Economist*'s than to Piketty's. Second, I haven't finished Piketty's book, although I spent some time exploring his data. Third, I'm no expert on macroeconomic policy or macroeconomic data.

Got all that? Doug Henwood provided a useful translation:

> So, I have a bias on a field in which I'm a naïf, and I'm going to comment on a book I haven't finished reading yet, but listen to me because I'm Nate Silver.

This, by the way, is a good time to clarify my use of terms like "centrist technocrat" and "technocratic liberalism." I've seen sharp people object to the way that many on the left use "technocrat" and "technocratic" in disparaging ways. After all, any number of leftie policy proposals, from a green jobs program to the Fully Automated Luxury Communism of our collective dreams, could only be carried out with the aid of *actual* technocrats—people put in key planning and coordinating positions because of their technical expertise. When I talk about "liberal technocrats," though, I'm not talking about urban planners and environmental engineers. What I mean, and what I take other leftist commentators to mean, is that the flawed worldview of some liberal pundits and politicians leads them to talk and think as if they *were* technocrats, devising non-political "solutions" to society's problems on the basis of their special expertise. That's a delusion. They're participants in a political struggle. They're not independent thinkers standing outside of the struggle between different ideological teams. They're Team Bourgeois Liberalism.

That Nate Silver belongs to this team has been clear for a long time, but it didn't bother me that much. He was a poll-cruncher and a popularizer of important ideas about statistics and probability, and he seemed to be doing good work in that capacity. I had a certain amount of hometown pride in the guy.

Unfortunately, by the time the 2016 election cycle rolled around, 538's need to generate clicks drove them to produce so much content that Silver was opining about the horse race every day. The proportions of "signal" and "noise" on 538 got pretty ridiculous—for a while there they were doing things like publishing the unedited transcripts of the editors chatting as they watched the primary election returns in various states.

In this context, Nate's political judgment started to get in the way of his primary mission. In the 2016 Democratic nomination battle, Hillary Clinton was desperate to triangulate between the increasingly left-wing expectations of Democratic primary voters and the far more realistic expectations of Democratic donors. She wanted to position herself as a "progressive who knows how to get things done" and not, as people like me (labeled "Bernie Bros" in mainstream media discourse) kept insisting, a corporate shill and a dangerous warmonger to boot. Silver repeatedly came to Secretary Clinton's defense, arguing that "the numbers" showed that she was about as "progressive" as Bernie.

In July 2015, for example, he wrote that "[t]he policy differences between the Democrats aren't all that profound; Clinton is pretty liberal...she and Sanders voted together 93 percent of the time in the two years they spent in the Senate together."

In one of those ridiculous chat transcripts—sorry, in 538's "live coverage" of the MSNBC Democratic debate in February

2016—he appealed to the same evidence to make the same point:

> If the policy differences between Sanders and Clinton seem relatively minor, that's because they are. The two of them voted the same way 93 percent of the time for the two years they were in the Senate together, according to research by Derek Willis.

He was taken enough with this factoid to repeat it later that night on his personal twitter account:

> Clinton and Sanders voted together the same way 93% of the time.

In a chat transcript that May, he granted that Clinton and Sanders were coming from "different places" ideologically, but still insisted that their policy conclusions were more or less identical, using the only piece of evidence he ever used to make this point:

> They voted together 93% of the time when in Congress together.

To spell out something that should be obvious, in the context of Senate voting records, there's room for entire worlds in a difference of seven percent. Imagine two Senators who served together for two years in 2001 and 2002 and voted together differently on only two occasions in that entire time (as opposed to Clinton and Sanders, who voted differently on dozens of issues in the same amount of time). Now imagine that the three votes were on the Patriot Act and invasion of Iraq...i.e. the de facto legislative abolition of the Fourth Amendment and a catastrophic war that led to decades of chaos and bloodshed in the Middle East. Would you describe those differences as inconsequential? How about if they'd voted the same way on those two issues but voted differently on a dozen or two minor procedural votes? Would they be more different in the first scenario or in the second one?

To see whether the 93% figure is telling or misleading, we need to look at how many of those votes were matters on which every member of the caucus voted the same way, or even trivial issues commanding broad bipartisan agreement. In acting as if the raw uninterpreted frequency of Clinton and Sanders voting together means much of anything in itself, Silver was acting like a caricature of a "data-driven" journalist.

Even the source of Silver's factoid, Derek Willis, said that "the 31 times Clinton and Sanders disagreed" in their two years in the Senate together "happened to be on some of the biggest issues of the day…"

Here are some of the votes on which they differed:

1. The war in Iraq—Sanders voted against the invasion and Clinton voted for it
2. A long series of votes to continue funding for the war which Sanders opposed and Clinton favored
3. A long series of trade deals which Sanders opposed and Clinton favored
4. The Patriot Act—Sanders voted against it and Clinton voted for it
5. Reauthorizing the Patriot Act—Sanders voted against it and Clinton voted for it
6. Guantanamo Bay—Clinton voted for a bill to force President Obama to keep the facility open by blocking funds for the transfer of detainees and Sanders voted against it
7. The Bank Bailout—Clinton supported it and Sanders opposed it

Significantly, some of the biggest ticket items on this list, like (1) and (4), don't even make it into Silver's factoid, because the 93% only covers the two years when they were both in the Senate. Bernie Sanders voted against the Patriot Act and the invasion of Iraq while he was in the House. Hillary Clinton voted for both as a Senator.

This brings us to the second problem with Silver's argument. He's committing the **Hasty Generalization** fallacy, and he's doing it in a particularly obvious and galling way.

Bernie Sanders has held elected office in one form or another since 1981. He's been in one or the other Houses of Congress since 1989. Hillary Clinton has been politically active either as an advisor to her husband or as a politician in her own right throughout the same period. As Doug Henwood has documented in his book *My Turn*, Clinton spent her years in Arkansas waging relentless war on the state's teachers' unions. (This is what her campaign bios were talking about when they said she "fought for better education in Arkansas.") She spent the 90s promoting NAFTA, harsher laws for criminal defendants, and draconian "welfare reform," all of which Sanders bitterly opposed.

The problem isn't just that Silvers's sample size is absurdly small. The two years in which Clinton and Sanders overlapped in the Senate were 2007 and 2008. You don't have to be a political junkie to recall that Senator Clinton spent most of that time doing something other than hanging out at her D.C. office and showing up for votes in the Senate. Presidential candidates are constantly faced with trade-offs between missed votes and missed campaign opportunities. Everyone understands this, and their colleagues make allowances for it. In those circumstances, the votes she would have been most likely to show up to were those that were most important to the Democratic Party's liberal base. Even so, she cast dozens of votes on the anti-Sanders side of "some of the biggest issues of the day."

Another example of "Hasty Generalization for Hillary" comes

from Kate Manne, a Philosophy Professor at Cornell University. In an April 2016 article in the Huffington Post, Manne suggests that both Sanders supporters' and right-wing Republicans' perceptions of Secretary Clinton were colored by misogyny:

> When Hillary Clinton behaves as other politicians do, or changes her positions, she is perceived as being more dishonest and as having less integrity. Yet as [former New York Times editor Jill] Abramson points out, Clinton has the highest rating on Politifact – reflecting the percentage of controversial statements that turned out to be true – of any politician in the race, Sanders included (in his case by a small margin).

Now, I certainly wouldn't deny that Manne has some basis for suspecting that misogyny influenced the views of Clinton critics who think she lacks integrity because she "lied about Benghazi" or because she won't admit that John Podesta is running a child sex trafficking ring out of the Comet Ping Pong pizzeria in Washington, D.C. But is this really the best explanation of the feelings of those on her left? Could it be that left-wing Clinton critics noticed that her attempt to reinvent herself as a "progressive who gets things done" was wildly out of step with her long history as a warmonger and corporate shill? Secretary Clinton was taking campaign money from the private prison industry right up until she realized that she needed to start talking about "mass incarceration" as a problem on the campaign trail. Given her record, I'd think that the simplest explanation of the perception that Clinton lacks integrity is that...she lacks integrity.

But what about the Politifact rating?

Put aside the obvious objection that when people talk about politicians being "dishonest," they aren't only or even primarily talking about those politicians *making false statements*. They're talking about making promises they don't intend to keep and paying lip service to causes on which they don't intend to waste any political capital and suddenly pretending to care about things their records clearly indicate that they don't care about.

A more basic problem is that Politifact isn't and doesn't pretend to be in the business of evaluating large randomized samples of the statements made by various politicians over the course of their careers. Those ratings are just raw percentages of those statements they happen to have evaluated. They're statistically meaningless.

To be fair, Manne might not have taken the time to look into Politifact's methodology. She's not a statistician. She's a philosopher and cultural critic who cited an interesting-looking factoid. Nate Silver, on the other hand, does this for a living. He should know better.

So why doesn't he?

This gets back to a larger point about the way that centrist ideologues rhetorically position themselves. If Silver had presented a substantive argument that Hillary Clinton really was pretty "progressive," he would have exposed himself as a participant in the ideological war who sees the world in a particular way and understands "progressive" politics in a particular way. As long as he can appeal to "the numbers," he can present himself as a disinterested technical expert.

The seventeenth century philosopher, logician, and mathematician Gottfried Leibniz often spoke of a future in which the tools of rational inquiry had become so advanced that philosophers would no longer need to dispute with each other. Instead, they would each sit down with pencils in their hands and say to each other, "Let us calculate."

That seems to be the 538 vision of politics. The problem is that not all moral and political disagreements stem from someone in one of the competing political factions forgetting to carry a one. Different people have different values, and different groups of people have different *interests*. To maintain the pretense that it can all be solved with calculation, then sooner or later you have to start cooking the books.

VI. Fallacies to Correct and a World to Win: Logic and Socialist Strategy

While we're on the subject of centrist Democrats—what the guys on Chapo would call "the libs"—this is a good place to plug Thomas Frank's book *Listen, Liberal: Or, What Ever Happened to the Party of the People?* I listened to the audiobook in the late spring and early summer of 2016, catching twenty minutes or half an hour at a time as I washed dishes or drove to class or walked the dog. It was written before the primary really got going, and the name "Bernie Sanders" is never mentioned, but Frank's book is a strikingly insightful guide to the distinction between the social democratic movement that coalesced around Bernie and the establishment wing of the Democratic Party that was then led by Hillary Clinton.

Frank's analysis isn't perfect. As indicated by the subtitle, Frank is basically a New Deal liberal. He thinks the Democratic Party was once the "party of the people." It wasn't. Franklin Delano Roosevelt was a canny ruling-class politician who understood that he had to throw the working class some concessions to keep popular discontent tamped down to manageable levels during the Great Depression.

There *was* a party of the people in that era. Its leader was Norman Thomas. FDR co-opted enough of the Socialist Party of America's short-term demands to stop it from growing to the point where it challenged the two-party system or threatened the capitalist order. (Asked what he thought about the fact that FDR had carried out much of his platform, Thomas quipped that "he carried it out on a stretcher.") When he wasn't making concessions to the working class, FDR was interning Japanese-Americans and sending back boatloads of refugees to Hitler's Europe and ignoring Eleanor's pleas for him to support anti-lynching legislation.

Frank's analysis of "what happened to" the Democratic Party also relies heavily on talk of something called "the professional class." Marxist critics might reasonably object that talking this way confuses the issue. The kind of "professionals" Frank is talking about might form a "caste," a distinct subgroup of the population with distinctive practices and attitudes and social codes, but they aren't a *class* if we understand social "classes" in terms of their relationship to "the means of production." (Doctors and lawyers who own their own practices are "professionals," but so are economists who work for universities.) Even so, Frank's analysis is useful and perceptive.

He traces the way that over the course of recent decades organized labor has steadily lost its "seat at the table" of Democratic politics. Again: Whatever Frank thinks, it was never a workers' party. In the "New Deal coalition," union leaders were definitely in the junior partner position relative to liberal capitalists, and those leaders often failed to meaningfully represent their own rank-and-file members. Even so, there's no denying that the economic policies of a President like Lyndon B. Johnson were what they were in part because LBJ represented a political alliance in which organized labor played a role. By the time of the Clinton Presidency, unions were at best an afterthought. Frank narrates the grim details of what that shift looked like both in D.C. and in the rustbelt.

More importantly, though, Frank's analysis isn't *just* about the way that the Clintonized Third Way-ized Democratic Party embodies the policy preferences of our corporate overlords. Instead, he focuses on that professional caste I talked about above. If you see everything from the perspective of their world of credentials and expertise, it makes sense to think of politics as just another profession. That's why liberals were always going on about how Hillary Clinton was *the most qualified candidate ever to run for President* and they were always mystified that no one else cared.

The policy preferences of the professionals end up lining up with the interests of the overlords in any case—Frank talks, for example, about the way that academic economists continually make false predictions about the good consequences of free trade pacts and continually sideline and dismiss critics of those treaties as "unserious"—but they do so in a particular way. "Seriousness" itself is central to the professionals' value system. "Ideological" ideas aren't serious ones. Think about Leibniz's vision from the end of the last chapter, and compare it to Obama's long and fruitless pursuit of a "grand bargain" with Republicans to slash and "save" entitlements. The correct policy "solutions" are the ones that will emerge from the smartest, best-credentialed people on both sides of the aisle taking off their ideological blinders and then just naturally converging on the "best" ideas. The "progressivism" of the contemporary Democratic Party is a form of liberalism that emerges naturally from this technocratic/ meritocratic worldview. Social injustice just *is* anything that blocks the best and the brightest from each race, gender, sexual orientation, and so on from rising to positions of power and prestige. Thus, the fact that so few CEOs are female registers with them as a "social justice" issue. Millions of men and women being put out of work by deindustrialization, on the other hand, isn't a matter of justice or injustice at all. It's just the economic equivalent of a natural disaster.

Socialists point out that the race to the bottom whereby businesses are moved from country to country in search of lower wages is something enabled by particular policy choices. Different choices would lead to different outcomes. Compare the industrial sectors of the American and German economies. The difference isn't that Germany is less technologically advanced. To the extent that deindustrialization really is driven by automation, socialists point out that in a different kind of economic system, technological advances could just mean that workers could vote themselves shorter shifts, working fewer hours for the same paycheck.

Professional caste liberals, on the other hand, mock Trump not just because his specific policies won't reverse deindustrialization but because "those jobs are never ever coming back." Everyone knows that the idea that a long-term trend could be reversed just isn't serious.

Even *easily understood* ideas are generally suspected of being unserious. Think about the difference between Bernie and Hillary on healthcare policy. Everyone knew where Bernie stood—"Medicare for All." You could be a complete political junkie throughout the 2016 election, mainlining thousands of hours of CNN and MSNBC directly into your bloodstream, and still not be quite sure what Hillary Clinton wanted to do to improve the Affordable Care Act. It should be improved upon, and she was going to improve on it…but to find out the details, you pretty much had to go onto her website and read a 150-page policy paper. On healthcare as on much else, the technocratic liberal message to the great mass of ordinary voters is, "We care about your problems. We're also much smarter than you, so you probably won't understand our solutions. Just trust us."

This isn't a winning message. (There's a reason that Donald Trump is President.) But what's the left's alternative?

When we're talking about social democratic reforms like Medicare for All, it's possible to build up mass support for these measures without expecting most people to be super-conversant with arguments than can be made for and against them. On a basic intuitive level, we can all understand that for-profit healthcare is horrible anti-human garbage.

In the long term, though, social democracy is not enough. When social rights like healthcare and education are won as reforms within the capitalist system, the current ruling class is kept in power. As we can see by looking at the transition from the New Deal/Great Society consensus of the mid-twentieth century to the Reagan/Clinton neoliberal consensus of the end of that century, that class can grant concessions to the rest of us for a generation or two and then move to roll them back again when they have a political opening to do so or when their profit rates fall and they have an incentive to take the political risk. The only long-term solution is to break from capitalism entirely—and to pull back from the environmental brink, we can't wait very long.

This, as we'll see in a moment, brings us back to logic.

Socialism is the movement for the working-class majority of the population to take charge of society. That's a vast undertaking. As we saw in our discussion of the Calculation Problem in Chapter III, it's far from obvious what a functioning post-capitalist economy would look like in practice. Winning socialism means (a) convincing a huge mass of people who don't currently think that anything but capitalism is possible that there even *can* be a different kind of world and that they should fight for one, and then (b) going through an immensely complicated process, full of pitfalls and problems, in which that enormous group of people figures out together how it can all work.

In her 1918 pamphlet on the Russian Revolution, Rosa Luxemburg wrote that "socialist democracy is not something which begins only in the promised land after the foundations of socialist economy are created; it does not come as some sort of Christmas present for the worthy people who, in the interim, have loyally supported a handful of socialist dictators." Socialism must be democratic both as means and as ends. For Luxemburg, this isn't a matter of moral idealism but of practical necessity. Radically democratic ends must be achieved by radically democratic means because *that's the only way socialism can happen.*

The tacit assumption underlying the Lenin-Trotsky theory of dictatorship is this: that the socialist transformation is something for which a ready-made formula lies completed in the pocket of the revolutionary party, which needs only to be carried out energetically in practice. This is, unfortunately – or perhaps fortunately – not the case. Far from being a sum of ready-made prescriptions which have only to be applied, the practical realization of socialism as an economic, social and juridical system is something which lies completely hidden in the mists of the future. What we possess in our program is nothing but a few main signposts which indicate the general direction in which to look for the necessary measures, and the indications are mainly negative in character at that. Thus we know more or less what we must eliminate at the outset in order to free the road for a socialist economy. But when it comes to the nature of the thousand concrete, practical measures, large and small, necessary to introduce socialist principles into economy, law and all social relationships, there is no key in any socialist party program or textbook.

Figuring all of this out means billions of people all around the world who are accustomed to taking orders from bosses and landlords and politicians learning to run their own workplaces and communities. That's going to be the biggest project of collective self-education in human history. It's going to have to involve multitudes of people engaging each other to discuss and debate different plans of action, different schemes of social organization, different solutions to a thousand problems that can't even be predicted from this side of society's democratic reorganization.

To have any hope of this gigantic collective debate being more than what William James called a "blooming buzzing confusion," a big part of this project is going to have to involve all these people learning to *carefully* and *precisely* reason with each other about their common tasks. This means, among other things, learning exactly where and how reasoning can go wrong so that we can learn together to do better. Making fun of nerds who care about logical fallacies can be funny. (I've admitted to being a fan of Chapo.) In the long run, though, if we're serious about the socialist project, we need to do better.

Postscript: 12 Rules for Reasoning

This book is about reclaiming logic for the left. That doesn't mean training leftists to go round for round with the Stefan Molyneuxs of the world in the game of mindlessly tossing the names of logical fallacies at each other like dung being thrown back and forth in the chimpanzee cage at the zoo.

One of the purposes of what I've written here is to explain what's wrong with this way of using logic and to try to model something better. Good reasoning isn't primarily about being loud and confident and good on your feet. Those are skills worth developing—as humans, we're built to respond to all of that—but those aren't the things that make people good *reasoners*.

The right-wing Logic Brigades give people the impression that caring about logic means dogmatically applying a few simple principles to everything and ignoring the fine-grained contextual differences between superficially similar situations. That's exactly wrong. If you actually care about getting the arguments right, you need to *slow the hell down* and pay attention to the subtleties.

In my exploration of the reasons that some leftists have learned to distrust logic, I laid part of the blame on the doorstep of my colleagues who teach introductory Logic and Critical Reasoning classes in ways that contribute to the problem. (I don't exempt myself from that criticism. My own techniques for teaching this material have evolved through trial and error and I'm very far from having figured it all out.) One colleague who I think *does* have a good handle on these issues is my friend Mark Warren. We went to graduate school together in Florida and we spent a lot of time drinking scotch and arguing about socialism and other subjects. I seem to have won the political argument—Mark is in DSA now—but he's convinced me of a lot more things than I've convinced him of over the years that I've known him. Here's something he had to say in an email exchange about this book:

> What I find with my students (and myself, often enough) is that they come away from arguments with just a general gestalt of how they work. I read Chomsky and have a warm feeling of endorsement. I read Shapiro and feel a buzz of cognitive dissonance, anger, revulsion at his strange little body. What I don't naturally have—what needs to be trained—is a clear picture of what they've just argued for, what points are crucial, and where a counterargument might start. I mock Shapiro because it's fun, but also because it's easier than rolling my sleeves up and showing myself and others why he's wrong.

So how do you do *that*? Let's end with a few tips.

1. *Carefully consider disanalogies.* Political arguments very often take the form of arguments by analogy intended to reveal inconsistencies. "You wouldn't be saying that if…" Rejecting all such analogies in a kneejerk way—"oh, that's just not the same at all"—is the equivalent of closing your eyes and putting your fingers in your ears and saying, "I'm not listening!" On the other hand, nodding along on the basis of superficial similarities is just as mindless. No two cases will be *completely* analogous. The question is always (a) whether the disanalogies are significant, and (b) if they're *relevant* to the point of the analogy. (See, for example, the discussion of Ben Shapiro's analogy between gender identity and age—and of Sophie Grace Chappell's much better analogy between gender identity and status as a parent—in Chapter II.) Being able to explain *how* and *why* they're irrelevant is a lot harder than either moralistically condemning someone for making an offensive analogy or just rolling your eyes and snarking about it, but it's worth the effort. Being able to explain

exactly why the two situations are relevantly different, such that the principle you're appealing to in one case really doesn't apply in the other, can help you gain a much deeper understanding of those principles and it can certainly help you explain them more clearly to others. Also, even just on a shaved-ape-dominance-game level, it's a much better move. If you never engage these arguments on their merits, listeners will get the impression that you aren't confident about the correctness of your position.

2. *Don't equate being good at critical reasoning with being "smart."* We use that word "smart" to refer to a lot of things—e.g. the ability to retain and recall pieces of information or the ability to quickly synthesize them—and at least some of those things are at least partially innate. Some people who are very "smart" in those senses are nonetheless very bad at making good arguments and detecting bad ones. Conversely, you don't have to have a great memory or be quick on your feet to learn the skills involved in good reasoning. For example...

3. *Learn to restate arguments in your own words.* This can help you see how the different parts fit together, and show where you can reasonably object to a premise or launch a counterargument. (See for example the repeated reconstructions of the Non-Aggression Principle—a crucial premise in many libertarian arguments—in Chapter III.) It also helps you think your way into the head of someone who sees these things differently than you do. If you want to be able to persuade such a person—or even someone on the fence between their view and yours—you need to be able to do that. Finally, by thinking about how *you* would put things, you can make sure that you're considering and responding to the best possible version of that argument—or at least the best one you can turn it into. As tempting as it can be to do this, knocking down

a poorly constructed *presentation* of an argument doesn't prove anything one way or the other about the underlying line of thought.

4. *Remember that not all good arguments have true conclusions and not all bad arguments have false ones.* Many perfectly good arguments fall short of **deductive validity**....and even valid arguments are only as good as their premises. (See Chapter III for a discussion of the distinction between **deductive logic** and **inductive logic**.) No matter how good you get at this stuff, it's not going to make you infallible. Sorry?

5. *Remember that inconsistencies can be resolved in multiple directions.* Let's say that, after carefully considering one of those "well, you wouldn't be saying X in analogous situation Y" arguments we discussed above, you decide that you actually *are* being inconsistent. That just means you got *something* wrong—that you hold a set of beliefs that can't *all* be true. That tells you nothing in itself about *what* you got wrong. Just because the person making the argument that convinced you that you're being inconsistent has his or her own ideas about how to resolve that inconsistency, that doesn't mean that this is the all-things-considered most plausible way to revise your views. (See the discussion of **Reductio Ad Absurdum** in Chapter I.) That brings us to...

6. *Inference to the Best Explanation is your friend.* (See the discussion of this reasoning method in Chapter II.) It can be easy to be seduced into accepting a set of ideas just because they all fit together in an interesting and internally consistent way, but that in itself is no guarantee that some other set of internally consistent ideas isn't better. You need to think carefully about which theory is simplest, which one explains the most, and so on. That means giving yourself time to think about it—the

opposite of the kind of snap judgments valorized by the online "logicbro."

7. *Mind the gap between "is" and "ought."* I've sometimes used the terms "moralism" and "moralistic" in negative ways here. I do think that the contemporary left sometimes falls into the trap of talking too much about the moral failings of individuals and forgetting that our role is to focus on bad *structures* and *systems*. One way or the other, though, trying to excise the language of *values* from our political arguments would be foolish. Remember our discussion of **Hume's Law** in Chapter II. A good argument for a normative conclusion (a conclusion about what people *should* do) has to rely on at least one (implicit or explicit) normative premise. Some political differences really are about how to achieve shared goals. (The intra-left argument about whether we should advocate a Universal Basic Income or a Universal Jobs Guarantee, for example, is probably like that. Different factual predictions about how things will play out might be enough to account for why people come to different conclusions.) Large-scale political differences, on the other hand—like the difference between socialists and right-wing libertarians—stem from the different sides caring about different goals. Speaking of which...

8. *Don't mistake competing values for logical inconsistency.* Politics and history and morality are all incredibly complicated. Sometimes it's legitimate to care about more than one goal. When those goals are in tension with each other, you have to make judgment calls. Depending on differences in what's at stake in different situations, the tradeoffs might be legitimately different. If Candidate A voted for the war in Iraq in 2002, and they're running against a primary challenger who opposed the war, that might be an excellent reason to favor the challenger. On

the other hand, if the anti-war candidate lost the primary, and the pro-war Democrat is running against right-wing Republican Candidate B who wants to abolish birthright citizenship and force all Muslims to wear yellow crescent badges, then the imperative to stop Candidate B might outweigh the general reasons we have to vote against candidates who supported the Iraq War and justify pulling the lever for Candidate A in a general election. The difference between someone who mistakes that for logical inconsistency and someone who can wade into the nuances is the difference between a person who uses logic-talk as a way of scoring points and someone who actually cares about good reasoning.

9. *Counterexamples are your friend.* You're considering an argument, and you can't decide whether the premises add up to a good reason to believe the conclusion. Here's a way to test it: Try to think about whether a structurally indistinguishable argument could get you from plausible premises to a conclusion that's obviously wrong. Or, similarly: You're considering a general principle—in all situations of type X, the right course of action is Y. Is this plausible? One of the best ways of showing that it isn't is to come up with a situation of type X in which the right course of action is pretty clearly not Y. This doesn't necessarily show that nothing in the neighborhood of the original principle is right—maybe it can be tightened up to avoid these cases—but it most definitely shows that anyone who wants to advocate it has more work to do to make it plausible. Speaking of which, and I really can't emphasize this one enough...

10. *Counterexamples are not arguments by analogy. Learn the difference.* Let's say that you're arguing with a libertarian. They object to redistributive taxation on the basis that it violates individual freedom. You might claim in response

that poverty leads to a lot of avoidable deaths and that saving lives is more important than respecting individual freedom. The libertarian then points out that, by that principle, the state should be able to harvest kidneys at gunpoint from unwilling citizens to transplant into the bodies of people who would otherwise die. There are several ways you could respond. One might be to go back to the drawing board and say that saving lives is more important than *minor* violations of individual freedom. You could then make the not-unreasonable point that violations of autonomy come in degrees, and that even on the (dubious) premise that rich people have some sort of moral right to every cent of their income, their autonomy is being violated a whole lot less by invading their bank accounts against their will than by invading their *bodies* against their will. That's a plausible response. Another— and I think this is the *best* response—is to say, "OK, you're right, I guess that's a bad principle, but let's talk about your conception of 'freedom.'" (See the discussion about competing notions of "freedom" from the end of Chapter II.) There are doubtless other reasonable leftist responses to be made at this point as well. But a frankly dumb response that's depressingly common in this situation is to accuse the libertarian of saying that taxation is *like* organ harvesting. They're not saying that. They're saying that your argument for taxation is a bad one—and they're right. Seriously, people. Don't do this. When you respond to a counterexample to a general principle by waxing indignant about how it's an offensive analogy, you're just revealing yourself as someone who doesn't understand how counterexamples work.

11. *Learn to think about what someone who didn't already agree with you would say so you can present the best version of your case.* The same set of skills involved in probing *other*

people's arguments for logical holes, looking at general principles in the premises to see if you can construct counterexamples to them, etc., can and should be turned on your own arguments before you make them. Realistically, as with almost everything in this list, no one is going to do a perfect job of carrying out this advice. (God knows I don't even consistently carry all of this out when I'm arguing with my conservative mother-in-law.) To the extent that you can train yourself to do this, though, you'll make much better arguments.

12. *Slow the hell down.* Learning the names of some fallacies is easy. Learning to reason well is hard. You need to really give yourself time to sit with arguments to think about how they work and whether the pieces fit together in a persuasive way. That's the only way to do this well.

An Alphabetical List of Logical Concepts Mentioned in the Book

(Plus A Couple of Bonus Ones I Couldn't Work In)

Ad Hoc Ergo Propter Hoc ("After it, therefore because of it") or the **False Cause Fallacy** (See Chapter IV): This is the mistake we make when we jump from the premise that Event A came before Event B to the conclusion that Event A *caused* Event B. "Bernie bashed Hillary in the primary, and then see what happened in the general—Trump won!"

Ad Hominem (Latin: "Against the man") (See Chapter I): This is the mistake we make when we treat an attack on the person making an argument as if it were a critique of the argument itself, as in, "Sally's case might be convincing if I didn't know for a fact that she's a crazy ultra-leftist who voted for Jill Stein."

Important Clarification: The *Ad Hominem* fallacy has nothing to do with rudeness or incivility. It can be committed in a polite, respectful tone. ("With all due respect, it's no surprise that you'd argue for an anti-capitalist position. You've had a hard life...") Conversely, people are often accused of *Ad Hominem* for saying mean things. This is incorrect. As long as you aren't treating the personal attack as if it counted as an objection to your interlocutor's argument, saying even vicious and disgusting things about them doesn't count as "committing an *Ad Hominem*."

Ad Populum (or **Appeal to the Masses**) (Not discussed in the book): This is like a populist version of **Appeal to Authority.** (See below.) It's the mistake we make when we treat the popularity of a position as a reason to believe that it's true (in the absence

98

of any particular reason to believe that most people will come to the right conclusion about the subject in question). This comes up enough on the left that this index would have been severely incomplete without it.

Appeal to Authority (See Chapter I): This is the positive version of *Ad Hominem*. It's the mistake we make when we treat the fact that the person making a claim is impressive or admirable (in some way that's irrelevant to their knowledge of the issue at hand) as if it counted as a reason to believe the claim. "Do you think that paranormal events aren't real? Well, the great writer Arthur Conan Doyle disagreed with you!"

Important Clarification: The *Appeal to Authority* fallacy isn't committed when you cite relevant expert opinion. It's not realistic to expect everyone to be knowledgeable about everything. If a discussion between two people who don't have any particular knowledge of details of climate science, "Almost all climate scientists believe that human activity is contributing to global warming" is a perfectly legitimate argument.

Appeal to the Masses: See **Ad Populum**

Appeal to Moderation: See **Golden Mean Fallacy**

Appeal to Hypocrisy: See **Tu Quoque**

Antecedent (Not discussed in the book): The "if" part of a conditional statement. For example, in the sentence, "If Bernie Sanders was the 2016 Democratic nominee, he would have won the general election," the antecedent is, "Bernie Sanders was the 2016 Democratic nominee."

Asserting a Disjunct (See Chapter IV): This is the mistake we make when we start from a **disjunction** (P or Q), assert one of the disjuncts, and conclude that the other one must be false. (Note that this is only a fallacy if the disjunction is *inclusive* rather than exclusive. For more on that distinction, see the entry on **disjunction**.) "Either we should organize at the grassroots or we should participate in elections. Grassroots organizing is crucial. So let's not bother with electoralism."

Asserting the Consequent (See Chapter I): This is the mistake we make when we reason from a **conditional** ("If P, then Q") and the **consequent** of that conditional ("Q") to the **antecedent** ("P"). An all-too-common form of this on the left has to do with "checking one's privilege." If Suzy is being blinkered by her privilege, that might lead her to advocate a certain position, but inferring from this conditional and the fact that Suzy *does* advocate that position to the conclusion that she came to the position by failing to take things into account that a less privileged person would have confronted is to fallaciously assert the consequent. Suzy might actually have perfectly good reasons—perhaps ones that have also convinced many less privileged people!

Begging the Question (See Chapter III): This is the mistake we make when we smuggle the conclusion of an argument into the premises and thus argue in a circle.

Composition Fallacy (See Chapter III): This is the mistake we make when we arbitrarily assume that the properties of an object will mirror the properties of its parts. "If the janitors go on strike, it'll be easy to replace them. After all, how hard is it to find a janitor?" When we explicitly spell out the argument, it's obvious that it's not deductively valid (and it's not a good argument in any other sense).

Premise One: It's easy to find a replacement for a single janitor who just quit.

Conclusion: It will be equally easy to find a replacement for a hundred janitors who walked off together.

So what's going on here? One way of thinking about this is that it's an **enthymeme** where people who deploy the argument typically aren't thinking about the implied background premise. Once that premise has been made explicit...

Premise Two: Whatever is true of each individual janitor will be true of a large well-organized group of janitors.

...we can see that we have no reason to believe it to be true.

Conditional (Not discussed in the book): A statement of the form "if P, then Q," which is expressed in the language of symbolic logic as P→Q. In this example, P is the **antecedent** and Q is the **consequent**.

Important Note: Thinking through the conditions under which conditional statements are true or false is surprisingly tricky. I didn't want to get side-tracked with this issue in the discussion of **Truth Tables** in Chapter IV, so I left out the table for conditionals, but this omission is corrected in the **Truth Tables** entry below.

Conjunction (See Chapter IV): The "conjunction" of two statements P and Q is the combined statement "P and Q," represented in the language of symbolic logic as (P ∧ Q).

Consequent (Not discussed in the book): The "then" part of a conditional statement. For example, in the sentence, "If Bernie Sanders was the 2016 Democratic nominee, he would have won the general election," the antecedent is, "He would have won the general election."

Deductive Logic (As Opposed to **Inductive Logic**) (See Chapter III): This is the kind of logic in which we evaluate arguments to see if they have valid logical forms.

Deductive Validity: See **Validity**

Denying the Antecedent (Not discussed in the book): This is the mistake we make when we reason from a **conditional** ("If P, then Q") and the **negation** of the **antecedent** of that conditional ("Not-P") to the **negation** of the **consequent** ("Not-Q"). In the language of symbolic logic, we represent this form of bad reasoning as:

$$P \rightarrow Q \: / \: \neg P \: // \: \neg Q$$

Disjunctive Syllogism (See Chapter IV): This is a valid argument form where the premises are a **disjunction** ("P or Q") and the **negation** of one of the disjuncts ("not-P") and the conclusion of the other disjunct. Since I'm writing this with my miniature schnauzer Lucy curled up next to me, I can't resist illustrating this by quoting from Andrew Aberdin's account of a debate at Cambridge University in 1615.

[T]he claim that dogs use logic was defended by John Preston (1587-1628) of Queen's College. "He instanced in a hound who hath the major proposition in his mind, namely, *The hare is gone either this way or that way*; smells out the minor with his nose, namely, *She is not gone this way*; and followed the conclusion, *Ergo this way*, with open mouth." The inference which the dog is purported to have followed is *disjunctive syllogism*, which we might abbreviate as "*P* or *Q*, not-*P*, therefore *Q*." Preston was answered by Matthew Wren (1585-1667) of Pembroke College, for whom dogs were distinguished by the excellence of their noses, not their reasoning: surely the dog determined the quarry's path by scent. While the moderator, Simon Reade of Christ College, agreed with Wren, the King [James VI of Scotland and I of England] took Preston's side, gave an example of a reasoning dog from his own experience, and suggesting that Reade should "think better of his dogs or not so highly of himself." Reade successfully mollified his sovereign with the suggestion that dogs that hunt by royal prerogative must be exceptions to laws that govern common hounds, and the debate concluded in good spirits.

Disjunction (See Chapter IV): The "disjunction" of two statements P and Q is the combined statement "P or Q," represented in the language of symbolic logic as (P ∨ Q).

> *Important Clarification*: In ordinary English, some disjunctions are "inclusive" (P or Q or both") and some are "exclusive" ("P or Q but not both") and we often rely on context to tell us which is which. To keep things simple, the logical disjunction symbol ∨ is always read "inclusively." If you want to write "P or Q but not both" in the language of symbolic logic, you have to write it out as (P ∨ Q) ∧ ¬(P ∧ Q). If you don't recognize those other symbols, see the entries for **conjunction** and **negation**.

Division Fallacy (See Chapter III): This is just the **Composition Fallacy** in the other direction. The arbitrary and implausible background premise mucking things up in this case is that the properties of each part of some larger whole will mirror the properties of the whole.

Enthymeme (Not discussed in the book): This is an argument where one or more premises are not explicitly stated, often because the premises being left out are too obvious to be worth spelling out. Think about, "Of course the flag has a color— it's red!" Technically, the conclusion doesn't follow from the stated premise, but in conversation with any remotely normal human being the extra premise that "red is a color" doesn't need to be explicitly stated. In contexts like that, you might as well leave them unstated. Life is too short as it is. On the other hand, sometimes when previously unstated premises are made explicit, we can see that we have no reason to believe them. See the entries on the **Composition** and **Division Fallacies** for examples of *that*.

Fallacy (See...every chapter): This is just a fancy name for a mistake in reasoning.

False Cause Fallacy: See **Post Hoc Ergo Propter Hoc**

Golden Mean Fallacy (or **Appeal to Moderation**) (Not discussed in the book): This is the fallacy of treating the mere fact that your position lies between two more "extreme" positions as if it gave us any reason whatsoever to think that your position is correct. Centrists do this all the time, of course, but so do lots of other people. There was a year of college when I had a Republican roommate who watched Fox News all the time. I saw Bill O'Reilly engage regularly in the rhetorical technique of quoting one or two viewer emails attacking him from the left and one or two attacking him for the same thing from the right. This was supposed to prove how reasonable he was, but the mere fact that some people disagree with you from one perspective and others disagree from another gives us no objective reason whatsoever to think that you got things right. Let's not just pick on the centrists and conservatives here, either: I've seen plenty of articles about intra-left disputes in socialist magazines that fell into this trap of treating the fact that the author's position happens to fall between two other positions as some sort of reason to believe that the author's view is right.

Hasty Generalization Fallacy (See Chapter V): A mistake in probabilistic reasoning where a conclusion is reached about a population on the basis of a sample of members of that population that isn't large enough or random enough to be sufficiently meaningful. If a Mayoral election is going on in New York City, a respectable poll would have hundreds of respondents. A sample of ten guys you find sitting at a particular bar in Brooklyn isn't big enough, and if they all came over to the bar together from a DSA meeting, this failure of randomness makes it even less likely that the proportion of the group planning to vote for each candidate will be representative of New Yorkers in general.

Hume's Law (HL) (See Chapter II): It is impossible (with some uninteresting exceptions described at the end of the chapter) to derive a normative conclusion (i.e. a conclusion about what *ought* to happen) from unmixed factual premises. "Fewer people will die if you push that man in front of the trolley" doesn't entail "you should push that man in front of the trolley" unless it's combined with the premise that "whatever leads to the fewest deaths is always the right thing to do."

Inductive Logic (As Opposed to **Deductive Logic**) (See Chapter III): This is the branch of logic where, instead of examining arguments to see if they are **deductively valid**, we examine them to see if they are inductively strong. See **inductive strength**.

Inductive Strength (See Chapter III): The equivalent of **validity** for **inductive logic.** Note that while validity is a binary concept — an argument is either valid, full stop, or invalid, full stop — inductive strength is a matter of degree. An argument is strong to the extent that the premises give the reader a good reason to think that the conclusion is true.

Inference to the Best Explanation (IBE) (See Chapter II): This is a particular kind of good (though not deductively valid) argument where you compare possible explanations of a given phenomenon and conclude that the one that's simplest, most elegant, most explanatory, and so on is most likely to be true. For examples, see...more or less all of biology, chemistry, physics, etc.

Law of the Excluded Middle (LEM) (See Chapter IV): Every statement is either true or false. In the language of symbolic logic, for every statement P, the following holds:

P ∨ ¬P

If you don't know what those symbols mean, see the entries on **disjunction** and **negation.**

Law of Identity (LI) (See Chapter IV): No statement can fail to be identical to itself. This is basically the application of the **Law of Non-Contradiction (LNC)** to the concept of identity.

Law of Non-Contradiction (LNC) (See Chapter IV): No statement is *both* true and false.

In the language of symbolic logic, for every statement P, the following holds:

¬(P ∧ ¬P)

If you don't know what those symbols mean, see the entries on **conjunction** and **negation.**

Logical Form (Not *explicitly* discussed in the book, but see Chapter IV): The "logical form" is what's left of an argument when you strip it down to Ps and Qs that can stand for anything. For example, the two arguments at the very beginning of Chapter IV are about two totally different subjects, but they share the same logical form, which is **Disjunctive Syllogism**: "P or Q, not P, therefore Q," or in the language of symbolic logic:

P ∨ Q / ¬P // Q

Modus Ponens (See Chapter I): This is the valid argument form where the premises are a **conditional** ("If P, then Q") and its **antecedent** ("P") and the conclusion is the **consequent** ("Q"). In the language of symbolic logic, we represent this inference as:

P → Q / P // Q

Modus Tollens (See Chapter I): This is the valid argument form where the premises are a **conditional** ("If P, then Q") and the **negation** of its **consequent** ("Not-Q") and the conclusion is the **negation** of its **antecedent** ("Not-P"). In the language of symbolic logic, we represent this inference as:

P → Q / ¬Q // ¬P

Negation (See Chapter IV): The "negation" of P is a statement of the form "not-P," represented in the language of symbolic logic as ¬P.

Non Causa Pro Causa (Or the **Questionable Cause Fallacy**) (See Chapter II): This is the mistake we make when we equate correlation with causation.

Questionable Cause Fallacy: See **Non Causa Pro Causa**

Tu Quoque (Or **Appeal to Hypocrisy**) (Not discussed in the book): This is the fallacy we commit when we go from the premise that someone is being hypocritical in saying P to the conclusion that P is false. Just because the pot is calling the kettle black, that doesn't mean that the kettle *isn't* black.

An important note of caution: When liberals (and some neoconservative Never Trump types) throw around accusations of "whataboutism," this *sounds* like an accusation of committing the **Tu Quoque** fallacy, but it often isn't clear that this is really what's going on there. Bob says, "We should be firing missiles at Russia to punish them for interfering in our election." Jane says, "Wait, hasn't the United States interfered in the elections of lots of other countries—including Russia—in much more severe ways? Should someone be firing missiles at us?" Bob then accuses Jane of "whataboutism." Is Bob legitimately accusing Jane of committing the **Tu Quoque** fallacy? I'm not so sure. It looks to me more like Bob is mindlessly using the accusation of "whatboutism" to shut down any attempt to apply consistent standards to the United States and its imperial rivals.

Truth Tables (See Chapter IV): This is a way of visually representing all the ways a certain kind of statement can be true or false. At the beginning of Chapter IV, there's a detailed breakdown of the truth tables for **negation, conjunction**, and **disjunction** and how you should read them. I left out the truth table for the **conditional** since I didn't want to get bogged down in a side issue. Here it is now, though:

$P \rightarrow Q$
T T T
T F F
F T T

F T F

If the **antecedent** (the "if" part) is true and the **consequent** (the "then" part) is false, the conditional statement as a whole comes out false and you write a little "F" under the conditional symbol. Otherwise, it gets a little "T."

In my experience, introductory logic students usually find the top two lines pretty intuitive and the bottom two confusing. Like most logic instructors, I've come up with some tricks to help people remember how this works.

Here's one: Krusty Burger sends you a coupon for a free burger. Think about different scenarios as equivalent to different lines of the truth table. First line: You bring the coupon to your local Krusty Burger and you get your free burger. The coupon worked as advertised. Second line: You bring in the coupon but they don't give you a burger. False advertising! Third and fourth lines: You don't bring it in, so whether or not you get a free burger, there's no issue of the coupon not working as advertised.

Or here's another one, suggested by a former student of mine at Rowan University in South Jersey: The conditional being false is like a student being absent from class. First line: Class meets today, and you're there. You're not absent. Second line: Class meets today, and you're not there. You are absent! Third and fourth lines: Class doesn't meet today, so whether you happen to go to the classroom or not, you can't be absent.

...but all of these are just tips for how to *remember* the truth table. They're not explanations of why it correctly represents what "if...then" means? So: Does it?

The unsatisfying but accurate answer is that the English

expression "if...then" is multiply ambiguous. The → of formal logic usefully represents at least some of what we mean by it in many contexts, and it can be used to represent truth tables that show us that (and why) **Modus Tollens** and **Modus Ponens** are valid and that (and why) **Asserting the Consequent** and **Denying the Antecedent** are invalid, but the messy complicated truth is that there are different kinds of conditional statements, a lot of which are true or false under circumstances we can't capture with an instrument as blunt as a truth table. For example, think about "counterfactual" conditionals, like "If Bernie was the nominee, he would have won." That one is almost certainly true. On the other hand, take, "If Martin O'Malley was the nominee, he would have won." Is that true? Probably, but it's a little harder to say. "If John Kerry had been nominated again in 2016, he would have won" is almost certainly false. (A feisty pseudo-populist like Trump would have wiped the floor with ponderous aristocratic Kerry.) Notice, though, that *all three* of those conditionals have false antecedents and false consequents. This tells us that the truth or falsehood of counterfactual conditionals isn't a simple function of the truth or falsehood of their component parts.

There is, unfortunately, a more general lesson here: Formal symbolic logic is a useful tool, but it isn't the alpha and omega of good reasoning. Sorry! This is why only a small slice of this book was devoted to formal symbolism and we spent a lot more time on informal fallacies and other broader issues pertaining to critical reasoning.

Validity (Or **Deductive Validity**) (See Chapters I, III and IV): A valid argument is one whose **logical form** makes it impossible for all the premises to be true without the conclusion being true. In normal circumstances, this is a desirable feature of arguments. After all, we don't want to be taken from true premises to false conclusions! On the other hand, some argument forms are technically valid for strange reasons. For one example, see the extended discussion of **Begging the Question** in Chapter III. For another, think about this argument:

Premise One: Douglas Lain is a hundred years old.
Premise Two: Douglas Lain is not a hundred years old.
Conclusion: The moon is made of green cheese.

Since it's logically impossible for both premises to be true, it's logically impossible for the premises to be true at the same time that the conclusion is false. However, if you *believe the conclusion* because you *believe the premises*, you've made some kind of mistake.

This gets back to the same point we ended up on in the discussion of **Truth Tables**:

Formal logic is a useful set of tools for avoiding certain kinds of mistakes that we can fall into as we try to reason about the world around us...but good reasoning isn't just a matter of mindlessly applying a few easy rules. Thinking like *that* is how you end up becoming the kind of logicbro social media troll who rattles off long lists of named fallacies in response to everything his interlocutors say. Actually becoming good at reasoning involves careful thought and attention and lots and lots of practice.

CULTURE, SOCIETY & POLITICS

Contemporary culture has eliminated the concept and public figure of the intellectual. A cretinous anti-intellectualism presides, cheer-led by hacks in the pay of multinational corporations who reassure their bored readers that there is no need to rouse themselves from their stupor. Zer0 Books knows that another kind of discourse – intellectual without being academic, popular without being populist – is not only possible: it is already flourishing. Zer0 is convinced that in the unthinking, blandly consensual culture in which we live, critical and engaged theoretical reflection is more important than ever before.
If you have enjoyed this book, why not tell other readers by posting a review on your preferred book site.

Malign Velocities
Accelerationism and Capitalism
Benjamin Noys
Long listed for the Bread and Roses Prize 2015, *Malign Velocities* argues against the need for speed, tracking acceleration as the symptom of the ongoing crises of capitalism.
Paperback: 978-1-78279-300-7 ebook: 978-1-78279-299-4

Meat Market
Female Flesh under Capitalism
Laurie Penny
A feminist dissection of women's bodies as the fleshy fulcrum of capitalist cannibalism, whereby women are both consumers and consumed.
Paperback: 978-1-84694-521-2 ebook: 978-1-84694-782-7

Romeo and Juliet in Palestine
Teaching Under Occupation
Tom Sperlinger
Life in the West Bank, the nature of pedagogy and the role of a university under occupation.
Paperback: 978-1-78279-637-4 ebook: 978-1-78279-636-7

Sweetening the Pill
or How We Got Hooked on Hormonal Birth Control
Holly Grigg-Spall
Has contraception liberated or oppressed women? *Sweetening the Pill* breaks the silence on the dark side of hormonal contraception.
Paperback: 978-1-78099-607-3 ebook: 978-1-78099-608-0

Why Are We The Good Guys?
Reclaiming your Mind from the Delusions of Propaganda
David Cromwell
A provocative challenge to the standard ideology that Western
power is a benevolent force in the world.
Paperback: 978-1-78099-365-2 ebook: 978-1-78099-366-9

Readers of ebooks can buy or view any of these bestsellers by
clicking on the live link in the title. Most titles are published
in paperback and as an ebook. Paperbacks are available in
traditional bookshops. Both print and ebook formats are available
online.
Find more titles and sign up to our readers' newsletter
at http://www.johnhuntpublishing.com/culture-and-politics
Follow us on Facebook
at https://www.facebook.com/ZeroBooks
and Twitter at https://twitter.com/Zer0Books